Premier English

for Nigerian Primary Schools

PUPIL'S BOOK **5**

Author
Nick Coates

Advisers
Olubunmi Olabisi Owoeye
Adedayo Olufemi Charles Aderibigbe
Susan Ayeni
Mohammed Bala
Okeke Okocha

MACMILLAN

Contents

1 Adire

Reading 1

Before reading: Look at the photograph. What can you see? How was the cloth made?

Adire is a traditional cloth made by Yoruba women in western Nigeria. An indigo dye is used which gives the cloth its special blue colour. A number of different ways of creating the designs are used – one of which is tie and dye.

Tie and dye

Tie and dye is simple and fun. You can do your own at home using any colours you like. The instructions below tell you how to make your own design using two different colours. You can even make your own colourful T-shirt!

You need:

- A piece of white cloth (or a white cotton T-shirt)
- String
- Dyes (one light and one dark colour, if you want two colours)
- Water (hot and cold)
- Plastic bowls for dyes and water
- Old newspapers
- Rubber gloves
- Stick
- Scissors
- Detergent

B Comprehension 1

1 Where is Adire cloth traditionally made? western nigeria
2 What colour is it? indigo
3 Is Adire always made by the tie and dye method? yes
4 Is tie and dye difficult? no
5 What colour cloth should you start with? blue
6 What colour dyes should be used? Any of your choice

C Reading 2

Before reading: How do you think you tie and dye cloth?

What you do:

1 Wash the white cloth and let it dry.

2 Tie the string tightly around the cloth. This will stop the dye colouring the tied areas. If you want a striped pattern, fold the cloth and tie all along the cloth (see diagram a). If you want a circular pattern, hold a centre spot and tie tightly below (see diagram b). To make more circles, make more ties below the first tie.

diagram (a) – a striped pattern   diagram (b) – a circular pattern

3 Prepare the workspace by covering the floor and worksurface with old newspapers.

4 Ask an adult to heat the water and mix the dyes in bowls. Rubber gloves should be worn when using dye.

5 Put the tied cloth in the light dye for five to eight minutes. Stir from time to time with a stick.

6 Remove when the colour is a little darker than you want. Rinse well in cold water. Don't untie the cloth yet.

7 Tie new string tightly to make new patterns.

8 Put the cloth in the dark colour and dye for five to eight minutes, stirring occasionally.

9 Remove the cloth and rinse in warm water, and then cold water.

10 Use scissors to cut all the string carefully.

11 The cloth should then be washed in a bowl of warm water with a little detergent. Then rinse in cool water before drying.

12 Clean all bowls immediately with hot water and detergent.

5

D Comprehension 2

1 Are these statements true or false?

  (a) The white cloth must be clean before tying. True
  (b) The string should be tied loosely around the cloth. False
  (c) The string is to stop the dye colouring tied areas. true
  (d) Diagram (a) shows you how to make circular patterns. False
  (e) The cloth should be put in the light dye before the dark dye. T
  (f) The cloth should be left in each dye for ten minutes. F
  (g) Cut off the string after the first dyeing. F
  (h) The cloth should be rinsed before cutting off the string. T

2 Why should the workspace be covered with old newspapers?
So you can protect your workspace

3 Why should you ask an adult to heat the water and mix the dyes?
So you shouldn't injure yourself

4 Why should you clean the bowls immediately you finish?
So it shouldn't stain

Word focus 🔍

Make sentences with these words:

create   design   pattern   fold   remove   rinse   stir   tightly
stripe   occasionally

E Grammar

1 Look.

Compare the active and passive sentences.
  You **tie** the string tightly around the cloth. (active)
  The string **is tied** tightly around the cloth. (passive)
  We **dyed** this cloth yesterday. (active)
  This cloth **was dyed** yesterday. (passive)
The passive is made using the verb *be* and the past participle.
It can be used in all verb tenses.

2 Write sentences. Use the words in brackets.
  (a) (the cloth/remove/after five to eight minutes)
  The cloth is removed after five to eight minutes.
  (b) (the cloth/wash/first)   (c) (string/tie/around the cloth)
  (d) (the water/heat/by an adult)   (e) (the dye/mix)
  (f) (the cloth/put/into the dye)   (g) (scissors/use/to cut off the string)

6

3 Look.

A sentence in the active or passive starts with the thing or person the sentence is about.

You should cover the workspace with newspaper.
(active: about what **you** do)
The workspace should be covered with newspaper.
(passive: about **The workspace**)

4 Make active and passive sentences.

(a) Yoruba women/Adire cloth/make

Yoruba women make Adire cloth.

Adire cloth is made by Yoruba women.

(b) you/tie and die/can do/at home

You ..*can tie*   Tie and dye ... *at home*

(c) rubber gloves/you/should wear/when using dye

You ... *should wear* Rubber gloves ... *when using dye*

(d) Mother/the baby/fed/an hour ago

Mother ... *fed*   The baby ... *an hour ago*

(e) this book/Chinua Achebe/write/in 1973

This book ...   Chinua Achebe ...

F Speech

1 Look and listen.

As we speak, our voice can rise or fall. This is called **intonation**.
When the voice falls at the end of what we say (falling intonation) it sounds finished. When the voice rises (rising intonation) it sounds like a question, or shows surprise. It is also used to sound more polite.

Wash the cloth.   Do you wash the cloth?

today   today   now   now

2 Listen and draw the arrows.

(a) newspaper   (b) newspaper   (c) colour   (d) colour

(e) scissors   (f) scissors   (g) water   (h) water

3 Talk about what you did in the holidays. You must talk for at least one minute without stopping. Prepare and practise in a group.

G Dictation

Listen to your teacher. Write the paragraph.

> Aminat and Atinuke are best friends. They are in the same class at school. Atinuke made a tie and dye T-shirt last week. Now she has agreed to teach Aminat. She has given Aminat a book about tie and dye.

H Composition

These pictures are from Atinuke's book about tie and dye.
Write one sentence (not more) for each picture to explain what to do.

(1)   (2)   (3)

(4)   (5)   (6)

(7)   (8)   (9)

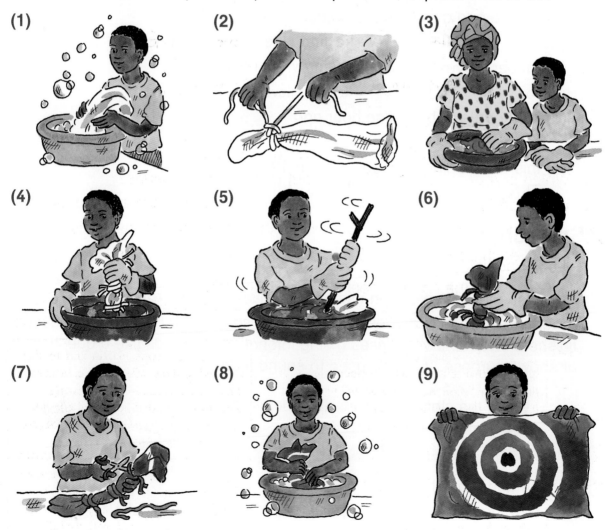

1 Wash the cloth first.

2 Using a dictionary

A Reading and comprehension 1

Before reading: What information can you find in a dictionary?

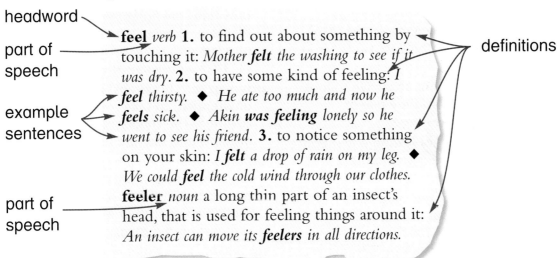

headword

part of speech

example sentences

part of speech

definitions

feel *verb* **1.** to find out about something by touching it: *Mother* **felt** *the washing to see if it was dry.* **2.** to have some kind of feeling: *I* **feel** *thirsty.* ◆ *He ate too much and now he* **feels** *sick.* ◆ *Akin* **was feeling** *lonely so he went to see his friend.* **3.** to notice something on your skin: *I* **felt** *a drop of rain on my leg.* ◆ *We could* **feel** *the cold wind through our clothes.*
feeler *noun* a long thin part of an insect's head, that is used for feeling things around it: *An insect can move its* **feelers** *in all directions.*

Look at the different parts of a dictionary entry.

1 Which part of the entry tells you how to spell a word correctly?

2 Which part of the entry tells you what the headword means?

3 Which part of the entry tells you how to use the headword in a sentence?

4 Which part of the entry tells you what sort of word the headword is?

5 Match each part of speech to its dictionary definition.

In a dictionary the part of speech is written *in italics:*

noun   verb   adjective   adverb   preposition

(a) _____ a doing word; a word in a sentence that tells you what happens: *In the sentence 'Musa opens his book and writes his name', the words 'opens' and 'writes' are both _____ that tell us what Musa is doing.*

(b) _____ words like 'in' and 'to' that are used to show where, when, how, etc.: *The _____ in the following sentences are underlined: I did it* <u>for</u> *you. She kept cheerful* <u>by</u> *whistling. Your books are* <u>on</u> *the table. I'll see you* <u>at</u> *one o'clock.*

(c) _____ a word that tells you more about a verb: *In the sentence 'She walks slowly', 'slowly' is an _____ which tells you how she walks.*

(d) _____ a word that tells you more about a person or a thing: *In the sentence 'He played with a big red ball', 'big' and 'red' are _____ that describe the ball.*

(e) _____ a word for a person or a thing: *'Sunday', 'egg', 'Ngozi' and 'shoe' are all _____ .*

9

Look at this page from a dictionary.

unscrew *verb* (**unscrews**; **unscrewing**; **unscrewed**) 1. to undo something by turning it: *Bola* **unscrewed** *the lid of the bottle.* 2. to unfasten something by loosening or removing the screws: *Mrs Okocha* **unscrewed** *the light switch from the wall.*

unsightly *adjective* not attractive to look at: *There was an* **unsightly** *pile of rubbish outside the house.*

unskilled *adjective* not having any special skills or training: *He is an* **unskilled** *worker and does not earn much.*

untidy *adjective* not tidy; in a mess: *Mary's bedroom was* **untidy***, with toys and clothes all over the floor.*

until *preposition* up to a certain time: *The shop is open* **until** *seven o'clock at night.*

unusual *adjective* not usual: *Kamal's eyes are an* **unusual** *colour.* ◆ *It's* **unusual** *for your father to be late.*

unwanted *adjective* not wanted or needed: *The Animal Shelter looks after* **unwanted** *animals.*

unwell *adjective* ill; not well: *Rotimi is feeling* **unwell** *and he has a headache.*

unwilling *adjective* not wanting to do something: *He was* **unwilling** *to go out, because he wanted to see a programme on TV.*

unwind *verb* (**unwinds**; **unwinding**; **unwound**) 1. to undo something that is wound up; to straighten something: *She* **unwound** *the hosepipe to water the plants.* 2. to relax: *My father likes to* **unwind** *with a cup of tea in front of the TV after a busy day at work.*

unwrap *verb* (**unwraps**; **unwrapping**; **unwrapped**) to take something out of its covering: *The children* **unwrapped** *the presents and saw the beautiful toys.*

up *preposition* 1. to a higher position; in a higher position: *Mary walked* **up** *the hill to school.* 2. towards someone or something or further along: *There is a cafe just* **up** *the road.*

up *adverb* 1. to a higher position; in a higher position: *Is the lift going* **up** *or down?* 2. out of bed: *Have you ever stayed* **up** *all night?* ◆ *It's 11 o'clock and Funmi isn't* **up** *yet.* 3. towards someone or something; as far as: *A taxi drove* **up** *and we got in.* ◆ *Count* **up** *to 100.*

upheaval *noun* (**upheavals**) a change that causes a lot of trouble or worry: *We were tired after the* **upheaval** *of moving house.*

uphill *adverb* going up a hill: *The bus slows down when it goes* **uphill***.*

1 Correct the spelling of these words.
   (a) unsigthly   (b) unskiled   (c) upheeval
   (d) unwiling   (e) unrapping   (f) upphil

2 What part of speech are these words?
   (a) unwanted   (b) until   (c) uphill   (d) unwrap

3 Some words have more than one meaning. Find a word with more than one meaning from the dictionary page.

4 Complete the sentences using a word from the dictionary page.

(a) The lorry was going very slowly as it went _____ .

(b) Sadiat is _____ . She has a headache and feels sick.

(c) This doesn't usually happen, it's very _____ .

(d) When we moved from Kano to Abuja it was a big _____ .

(e) My mother is always angry if I am _____ when I leave our house.

C Grammar

1 Join the sentences to make one sentence. Use **who**, **which** or **that**.

> We can join sentences with the relative pronouns **who**, **which** or **that**.
> *I met the man **who** painted that picture.*
> Use **who** for people and **which** for things. Use **that** for both people and things.

(a) A dictionary is a book. It gives the meanings of words.
  A dictionary is a book which gives the meanings of words.

(b) A cheetah is an animal. It runs very fast.

(c) My teacher is a kind person. She helps all her pupils.

(d) A bee is an insect. It stings.

(e) Yesterday I met a boy. He knows your sister.

(f) I've found my English book. I lost it last week.

(g) They played a lot of music. It was very loud.

(h) Here is the dictionary. You asked me to buy it.

(i) This book is very interesting. You gave it to me.

(j) Aminat has a friend. She always helps her.

2 Make ten sentences from the table. Complete them about yourself.

I	like	people	
		animals	who
		games	which
	dislike	books	that
		films	

I like animals that are friendly.

D Speech

1 Look.

> **Wh-** questions use a question word (**Who**, **What**, **Where**, **How**, etc.) and ask for information. Use **falling intonation** with these questions.
>
> *Where do you live?*   *How old are you?*
>
> **Yes/no** questions do not contain question words and they ask for a **Yes** or **No** answer. Use **rising intonation** with them.
>
> *Do you live in Bauchi?*   *Are you ten years old?*

Complete the questions with words of your own. Draw arrows to show the intonation.

(a) Is this your _____ ?   **(b)** When is your _____ ?

(c) Where do you go to _____ ?   **(d)** Can I borrow your _____ ?

(e) How many _____ have you got?   **(f)** Does your family live in _____ ?

2 Ask and answer your questions in pairs.

3 Read what Atinuke and Usman are saying about this new school year.

> This year I'm going to work hard. I'm going to read a lot of books and I'm going to do all my homework.

> I want to learn a lot this year. I intend to do well in all the tests.

Now say what you are going to do this year.

I'm going to ...   I intend to ...

I want to ...

E Dictation

Listen to your teacher. Write the paragraph.

> Aminat has a twin brother. His name is Usman. He is also in the same class at school. Aminat and Usman have thought about what they want to achieve this year at school. They both want to do very well.

F Composition

1 Write a letter to a friend. Tell your friend what you want to achieve in school this year.

2 Below are nine sentences about *My best friend.* Write the sentences as a text with three paragraphs.

> When we write a text we divide it into **paragraphs**. Each paragraph is about one idea or topic.

- The first paragraph should be about the friend's **personal details**.
- The second paragraph about what she looks like (her **appearance**).
- The third paragraph about her **family**.
  - (a) Decide which of the sentences should go into each paragraph. (There are three sentences in each paragraph.)

Paragraphs

Personal details	Her appearance	Her family
3,		

(b) Put the sentences into the best order.

(c) Write the text in your exercise book.

Sentences

1 She is ten years old.
2 Ngozi's father is a doctor.
3 My best friend's name is Ngozi Obani.
4 She has short braided hair.
5 She has three brothers and two sisters.
6 She lives in Enugu.
7 Her mother is a nurse.
8 Ngozi is tall and dark with beautiful eyes.
9 She likes to wear colourful clothes.

Fun box

Can you answer these?

1 Which common English word is usually pronounced incorrectly?
2 Which word of five letters is pronounced the same if you take away the first, third and last letters?

3 Two letters

Reading 1

Before reading: Look quickly – who is the letter to and who is it from?

> 39 Nyerere Road
> Goldfield Estate
> Abuja
> 27 September
>
> Dear Aminat,
>
>   I'm sorry I didn't come to your birthday party last Saturday. Are you angry with me? Please don't be!
>
>   I was really looking forward to the food, the games and the dancing when I fell ill with measles. I started with a runny nose and my eyes were red and hurt in the light. I also had a cough, felt hot and was tired. Then I got a rash. I still wanted to attend the party but the doctor told Mummy that it was infectious.
>
>   I tried three times to phone you but your line was busy. I'll try and call you again before the end of the week. I hope you understand.
>
>   I already feel better. The rash has gone but I still have to stay in the house for five more days.
>
>   It's boring at home and I can't wait to see you. I hope you kept some sweets and cakes for me. You ought to! I've bought you a present.
>
>   So how does it feel to be ten?
>
> See you soon,
> Atinuke

B Comprehension 1

1 What is Atinuke's address?
2 When was the letter written?
3 Why did Atinuke want to go to the party?
4 Why didn't Atinuke attend the party?
5 What happened to Atinuke when she got measles?
6 What did the doctor tell Atinuke's mother?
7 Can Atinuke go out yet?
8 How old was Aminat on her birthday?

C Reading 2

Before reading: How is the layout of the letter below different from Atinuke's letter?

39 Nyerere Road
Goldfield Estate
Abuja

27 September 2005

The Principal
St John's Primary School
Goldfield Estate
Abuja

Dear Madam,

Atinuke Idowu

This is to inform you that our daughter is unable to attend school because she is sick with measles.
As the illness is infectious, we would like to keep her at home until she has fully recovered. This will be a further five days so she will not return to school until next week.
We would appreciate it if you could inform her class teacher.
Many thanks for your understanding.

Yours sincerely,

Adebayo Idowu

Adebayo Idowu (Mr)

D Comprehension 2

1 Whose address is at the top right?
2 Whose address is below on the left?
3 What is the address of Atinuke's school?
4 Who is the letter from?
5 How does Mr Idowu address the principal?
6 What is the heading of the letter?
7 What does Mr Idowu tell the school principal in this letter?
8 When will Atinuke return to school?

Word focus

Make sentences with these words:

measles   cough   rash   infectious   attend   inform   unable   appreciate

15

E Grammar

1 Look.

> Use **must** or **have to** for a rule or something which is very important to do.
> Use **must not** for the negative.
>
> > *You **must** be quiet in assembly. They **had to** visit their uncle in hospital.*
> >
> > *Atinuke **mustn't** go out because measles are infectious.*
>
> Use **should** or **ought to** for something which is a good idea to do. Use
> **should not** or **ought not** to for the negative.
>
> > *We **should** ring Atinuke who is ill.   We **ought to** send her a present.*
> >
> > *We **shouldn't** visit her because we could catch measles.*
>
> **Must** and **have to** are stronger than **should** and **ought to**.

2 Complete the sentences with your own ideas.

(a) Children must ...

(b) Teachers have to ...

(c) Parents ought to ...

(d) I should ...

(e) At school we mustn't ...

(f) My friends and I shouldn't ...

3 Write six sentences about your favourite sport or game. Use **must**,
mustn't, **have to**, **should**, **shouldn't**, **ought to** or **ought not to**.

In football, players mustn't touch the ball with their hands (except the goalkeeper).

F Speech

1 Look.

When you speak to someone, you must use the correct level of formality.
- If you speak to an older person in the same way that you speak to a friend, it will show a lack of respect.
- If you speak to a friend in a very formal way, it will sound silly and show you do not know English well.

2 Match the formal and informal ways of saying the same thing.

Informal	Formal
(a) Hi! How're you?	(i) Could you please tell me where the bus station is?
(b) I want that.	(ii) Goodbye.
(c) Can I go now?	(iii) May I have that, please?
(d) Where's the bus station?	(iv) Good morning. How are you today?
(e) Bye.	(v) Would you mind if I left now?

3 Read what the girls said in these two situations. Were they correct?

Hello doc! I'm feeling great now and I want to go to school. That's OK, isn't it?

I'm delighted to see you again. I hope you have fully recovered from your illness.

What should they have said?

G Dictation

Listen to your teacher. Write the paragraph.

When you have measles you should rest and stay inside. It is infectious so other children can catch it from you. However, you can only catch measles once. After you have had the illness you will never catch it again.

H Composition

1 The diagram below shows the layout of a formal letter. Match the items in the box to the numbers in the diagram.

opening of letter (*Dear* ...)	heading	sender's full name
the contents of the letter	date	signature
receiver's address	sender's address	closing of letter (Yours ...)

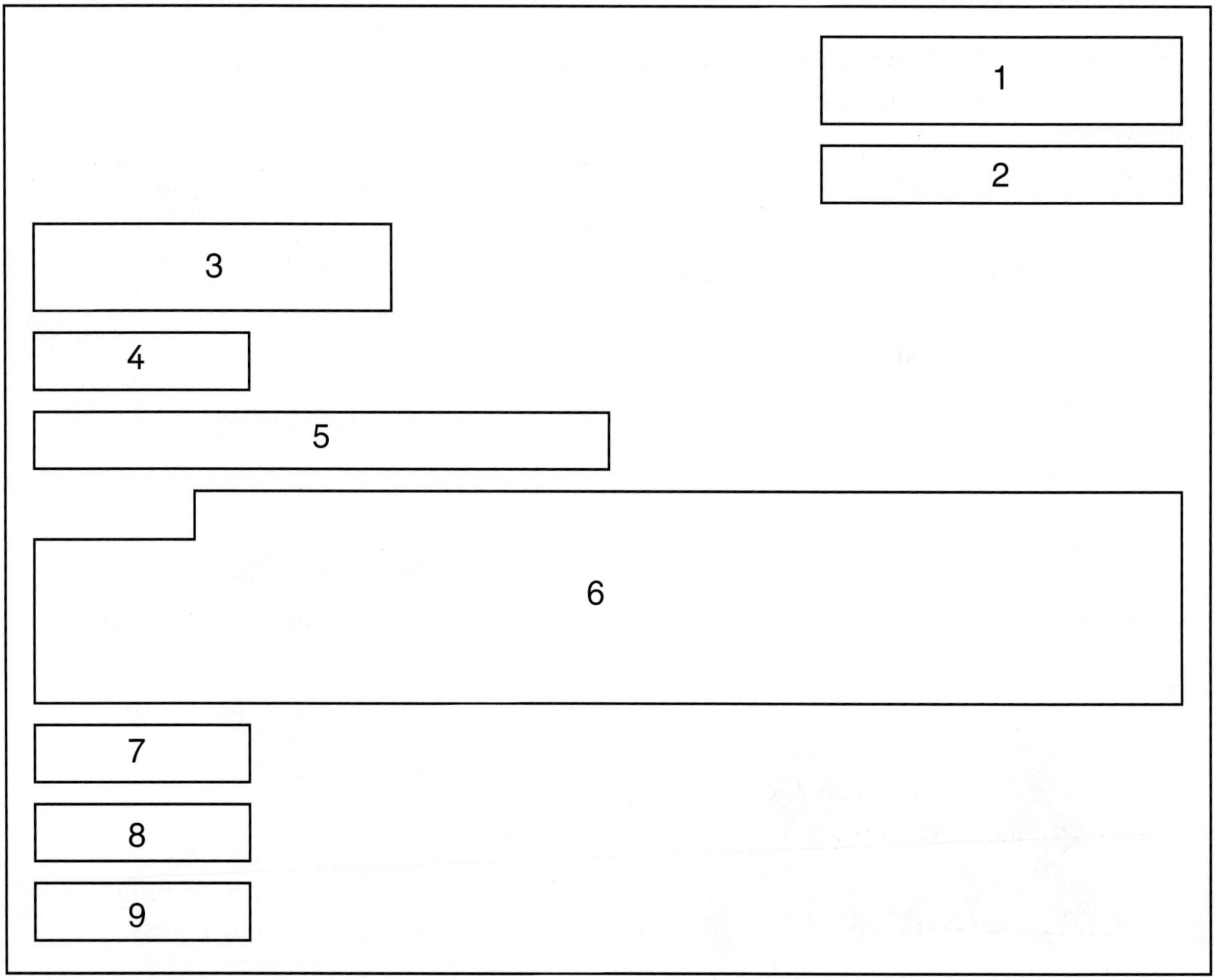

1

2

3

4

5

6

7

8

9

2 Write a formal letter.

Mr Idowu has to write again to the principal of Atinuke's school. It is 4th October. Atinuke is still ill and cannot return to school. Use the following as the contents of the letter:

This is to inform you that our daughter will not be returning to school today as hoped. She has not yet recovered from her illness.

She will see the doctor again tomorrow and we hope she will be able to attend school on Wednesday of this week.

4 On the telephone

A Reading 1

Before reading: Do you often use the telephone? Who do you talk to?

Atinuke needs some help with her homework. She phones some people.

1 *Phone rings.*

Aminat: Hello, Aminat Buhari speaking.

Atinuke: Hello, Aminat. It's Atinuke. How are you?

Aminat: I'm fine, thanks, Atinuke. And you?

Atinuke: Great! Listen, Aminat. I've got a problem with my homework.
Do you know when Ghana became independent?

Aminat: Sorry, I've no idea but Chike might know.
Why don't you call him?

Atinuke: I will, thanks. Bye.

Aminat: Bye.

2 *Phone rings.*

Mrs Okocha: 532175, can I help you?

Atinuke: Hello, ma. It's Atinuke here. Could I speak to Chike, please?

Mrs Okocha: I'm sorry, Atinuke. He's gone out with his grandfather. Can I take a message?

Atinuke: Yes, please. Could you ask him to phone me when he gets home?

Mrs Okocha: Of course.

Atinuke: Thank you. Goodbye.

Mrs Okocha: Goodbye.

B Comprehension 1

1 Who does Atinuke call first?

2 What does Atinuke want to know?

3 Does Aminat know the answer?

4 Who does Atinuke call next?

5 What is Chike's telephone number?

6 Does Atinuke speak to Chike?

7 Where is Chike?

8 What message does Atinuke leave for Chike?

C Reading 2

Before reading: What do you think Chike will say when he calls back?

1 *Phone rings.*

Mrs Idowu:	Bukola Idowu.
Chike:	Good morning, ma. It's Chike here. Atinuke asked me to phone her.
Mrs Idowu:	Hello, Chike. I'll call her.
Chike:	Thank you.
	[*pause*]
Atinuke:	Hi, Chike. Thanks for phoning me back.
Chike:	That's OK. What do you want?
Atinuke:	I need to know when Ghana became independent for my homework. Do you know?
Chike:	I don't, but my father used to live in Ghana. You can ask him. He's at his office but you can call him there, he won't mind.
Atinuke:	OK, what's his number?
Chike:	432771. He works at the Independence Hospital.
Atinuke:	432771, thanks Chike. Goodbye.
Chike:	Good luck, bye.

2 *Phone rings.*

Man:	Hello, Tukur and Yusuff.
Atinuke:	Oh, is that 432771?
Man:	No, this is 432774.
Atinuke:	I'm sorry. I've dialled the wrong number.
Man:	That's alright. Goodbye.

3 *Phone rings.*

Woman:	Good morning, Independence Hospital. How can we help you?
Atinuke:	Good morning, could I speak to Mr Okocha, please?
Woman:	Certainly, who is calling?
Atinuke:	Atinuke Idowu.
Woman:	I'll put you through.
	[*another phone rings*]
Mr Okocha:	Good morning, Chinedu Okocha.
Atinuke:	Hello, Mr Okocha. This is Atinuke. Chike gave me your number.
Mr Okocha:	Yes, Atinuke. How can I help you?
Atinuke:	I need to know what year Ghana became independent. Do you know?
Mr Okocha:	Yes, it was in 1957.
Atinuke:	Thank you very much, Mr Okocha. Goodbye.
Mr Okocha:	Goodbye, Atinuke.

D Comprehension 2

1 Does Chike call Atinuke?

2 Does Chike know the answer to Atinuke's question?

3 Who will know the answer?

4 What is Chike's father's phone number?

5 What is the telephone number of Tukur and Yusuff?

6 What does Atinuke say when she understands she has made a mistake?

7 What is the answer to Atinuke's homework question?

Word focus

Make sentences with these words:
independent   message   dial   put someone through

E Grammar

1 Look.

> Use **may** or **might** to talk about possibility.
>
> *Chike **might** know.*   *It **may** have been in 1957, but I'm not sure.*
>
> Also use **may not** or **might not** for negative possibility. However, you cannot use them in questions.
>
> *Usman might not know.*

2 Rewrite the sentences. Use **may**, **might**, **may not** or **might not**.

(a) Perhaps Aminat's mother knows.   *Aminat's mother may know.*

(b) Perhaps we can find the answer in a book.

(c) Perhaps my brother won't know.

(d) Perhaps Usman is not at home.

(e) Perhaps it will rain.

(f) Perhaps it won't be so hot today.

3 Look. Then ask and answer Atinuke's question.

> I might be a doctor or I might be a nurse.

> What are you going to be when you grow up?

> I don't know. I may be a pilot.

21

4 Write sentences about the children. Use the words next to the pictures.

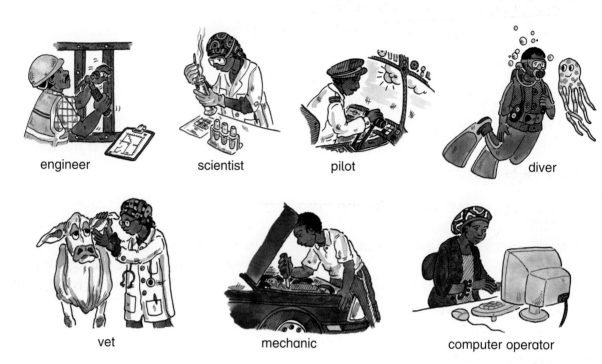

engineer   scientist   pilot   diver

vet   mechanic   computer operator

(a) Usman likes planes.   *He may be a pilot.*

(b) Chike likes cars.   **(c)** Yemi likes animals.

(d) Ahmed likes building things.   **(e)** Bukola likes swimming.

(f) Uchenna likes computers.   **(g)** Zainab likes science.

F Speech

1 Find sentences in the conversations on pages 19 and 20 and practise saying them. You must always be polite on the telephone.

(a) What you say when you answer the phone.

(b) What you say to introduce yourself when you call and it is answered.

(c) What you say to offer to take a message.

(d) What you say to leave a message.

(e) What you say when you want to talk to someone else.

(f) What you say when you dial a wrong number.

2 Practise conversation 4 on page 20 in pairs.

Use heavy stress (say a word or syllable louder) to correct someone.

Is that Mallam Musa?   *No, it's Mallam **Kolo**.*

Is that 745139?   *No, it's 745**2**39.*

3 Work in pairs and act out telephone conversations. One of you is A and one of you is B. Sit back-to-back.

(a) A calls B. B answers. They are friends.

(b) B calls A. B asks to speak to C.

(c) A calls B. A leaves a message for C.

(d) B calls A. B is returning a call.

(e) A calls B. It is a wrong number.

G Dictation

Listen to your teacher. Write the paragraph.

> Chike is Usman's best friend. He is in the same class at school as Usman, Aminat and Atinuke. They often telephone each other to ask for help with homework or to arrange a meeting. They often visit each other to play games or watch television together.

H Composition

1 Put the sentences in the correct order. Write the telephone conversation.

Chike:	Thank you. Goodbye.
Chike:	Hello, Mallam. It's Chike here. Could I speak to Usman, please?
Mallam Buhari:	I'm sorry, Chike. He's gone out with his sister. Can I take a message?
Mallam Buhari:	Goodbye, Chike.
Chike:	Yes, please. Could you ask him to phone me when he gets home.
Mallam Buhari:	Of course.
Mallam Buhari:	778341, Mallam Buhari speaking. Can I help you?

2 Work in pairs. Write *two* of your conversations from Speech 3 above.

Fun box

Did you know ...?

... in telephone numbers we say 0 as 'zero'.

... we usually say the same number repeated as 'double'. 66 is 'double six'. So 6663004 is 'double six six, three double zero, four'.

5 Polite Tortoise

A Reading 1

Before reading: What stories do you know about Tortoise? What tricks does he play?

Once upon a time, Tortoise was walking along when he got a thorn in his foot. "Ouch!" he cried. "Now I can't walk. What shall I do?"

After a while, an old woman passed by. Tortoise politely asked her for help. "Excuse me, Madam. Could you help me, please? Could you pull a thorn out of my foot?"

The old woman smiled and bent down. She found the thorn and quickly pulled it out. Tortoise thanked her and they both went on their way.

However a minute later, Tortoise had an idea. He called after the old woman, "Excuse me, where's my thorn, Madam?"

"I don't know," answered the woman. "I threw it in the bush."

Tortoise began to cry, "Oh, no! My thorn is lost. What am I going to do?"

The old woman felt sorry for Tortoise and said, "Please, don't cry. Here's an egg for you."

Tortoise was very pleased. He took the egg and walked on to a village. He knocked on the door of a house and a man answered it.

"Please, Sir," said Tortoise politely, "may I stay the night with you? It's late and cold."

"Yes, of course you may. Please come in," said the man.

B Comprehension 1

1 Why couldn't Tortoise walk?
2 Who helped him?
3 What did she do?
4 What did Tortoise ask the old woman to give him?
5 Did Tortoise really want the thorn?
6 Why did Tortoise cry?
7 What did the old woman give Tortoise?
8 What did Tortoise want from the man in the village?

C Reading 2

Before reading: What do you think Tortoise will do next?

Tortoise went into the man's house. "Can I put my egg on this plate?" he asked.

"Yes, of course you can," answered the man.

In the night Tortoise got up quietly and ate the egg. In the morning Tortoise thanked the man. As he was leaving, he asked the man, "Where's my egg? I left it on the plate."

"I don't know," answered the man. He searched his house but he couldn't find the egg.

Tortoise began to cry, "Oh, my beautiful egg! It's gone! I'm sure your cat ate it in the night."

The man felt sorry for Tortoise and said, "Don't cry. I'm sorry for your loss. Here's a hen for you."

Tortoise took the hen and left feeling very pleased with himself.

The next evening Tortoise arrived at another village. He met a young woman outside her hut.

"Good evening," he said. "Could I stay the night with you, please? I'm tired and it's so cold outside."

"Come in, Tortoise, and you can leave your hen with my goat," she answered.

D Comprehension 2

1 Where did Tortoise put his egg?
2 What did Tortoise do in the night?
3 Why did he eat it?
4 Who did Tortoise blame for his loss?
5 What did the man give to Tortoise?
6 Was Tortoise happy?
7 What did Tortoise want from the young woman?
8 Where did he leave his hen?

Word focus

Make sentences with these words:

thorn   pass by   bend down   feel sorry   search   loss   blame

1 Look.

> Use **can** and **could** for polite requests. **Can** is more informal.
>   *Can you tell me the time, Chike?*
> **Could** is more formal. Use it with older people and strangers.
>   *Could you help me, please?*

2 Make polite requests.

(a) Help with homework (a friend) Can you help with my homework?

(b) Help with homework (a teacher) Could you help with my homework, please?

(c) Tell me the time (a friend's father)

(d) Pass me the salt (a young sister)

(e) Lend me a dictionary (a friend)

(f) Give me a sweet (a brother)

(g) Tell me where the hospital is (a stranger in the street)

(h) Play football with me (an uncle)

3 Look.

> Use **can**, **could** and **may** to ask for permission. **Can** is informal. **Could** is more formal. **May** is the most formal.

4 Rewrite the sentences. Use **can**, **could** or **may**.

(a) I want to use your phone. (to a friend) Can I use your phone?

(b) I want to speak to Mr Okocha. (to a stranger on the phone)

(c) I want to leave a message. (to a friend's mother on the phone)

(d) I want to use your bike. (to a young sister)

(e) I want to leave the classroom now. (to a teacher)

(f) I want to go to a friend's birthday party. (to your father)

(g) I want to come in. (a friend)

5 Rewrite this dialogue. Use polite formal language.

A: Help me!

B: What?

A: I've lost my shoe. Find it quickly.

6 Work in pairs. Act out your two dialogues.

F Speech

1 Look.

> Intonation is very important if you want to sound polite in English.
> The polite intonation pattern is fall then rise at the end.
>
> *Could you help me, please?*

2 Practise the requests and permission sentences you wrote in Grammar above. Use polite fall–rise intonation.

3 Complete the story of 'Polite Tortoise'. Work in a group.
- What will Tortoise do in the night?
- What will he say to the young woman?
- What will the young woman do?
- What will Tortoise do next?
- Will Tortoise be successful with his tricks or will he be taught a lesson?
- What will happen at the end of the story?

4 Tell your story to another group.

G Dictation

Listen to your teacher. Write the paragraph.

> It is very important to be polite. However, it is not sufficient to be polite. If you have bad intentions, being polite does not make you good. Tortoise in the story is very polite but he is up to his old tricks. He cheats all the people he meets.

H Composition

Complete the story of 'Polite Tortoise'. Write the story you discussed in the Speech above.

Fun box

Did you know ...

... a tortoise lives a very long time.
This tortoise is older than you.
It is about a hundred years old.

6 Tortoise pays the price

A Reading 1

Before reading: Tell the story of 'Polite Tortoise' so far.

Tortoise left his hen with the goat and went to bed. In the night he got up, went to the place where the goat was and ate the hen. He left the bones next to the goat.

In the morning he asked the young woman for his hen. There was no hen, of course. Tortoise started to cry again, "My hen, my beautiful hen! Your goat ate it in the night."

The woman felt sorry for Tortoise so she gave him the goat to replace the hen. Tortoise thanked the woman and quickly left the village.

Later Tortoise arrived at a farm and found the farmer. He asked the farmer if he could stay at his farm. He explained that he was very tired. The farmer invited him in. Tortoise asked the farmer where he could leave his goat.

"You can leave it next to my son's bed," the farmer answered. "He will look after it for you."

As you have guessed, tricky Tortoise got up in the night and ate the goat. He put the bones on the boy's bed. In the morning he thanked the farmer and asked for his goat. When they looked on the boy's bed they found only the bones.

B Comprehension 1

1 Put these events in order:

   (a) Tortoise asked for the goat.

   (b) Tortoise met a farmer.

   (c) Tortoise was given a goat.

   (d) Tortoise left the bones with the goat.

   (e) Tortoise asked for the hen.

   (f) Tortoise ate the goat.

   (g) Tortoise left his goat with the boy.

   (h) Tortoise ate the hen.

   (i) Tortoise left the bones with the boy.

   (j) Tortoise left his hen with a goat.

2 Why did Tortoise leave the bones of the hen with the goat?

3 Why did Tortoise cry when they found the hen's bones?

4 Why did Tortoise leave the goat's bones with the farmer's son?

5 Do you think the farmer will believe Tortoise?

C Reading 2

Before reading: How do you think the story will end?

Now, read quickly and put the four sections in the correct order.

(a) However, Tortoise was greedy and he wasn't polite anymore. He spoke rudely to the farmer, "No, I don't want your cow. Give me your son!"

The farmer thought for a minute and then he said, "OK. Wait outside, I'll bring the boy to you."

(b) "This is a very heavy boy," Tortoise thought. "Or perhaps the man has tricked me and it's only stones! I'd better open it to see."

So Tortoise opened the sack and the farmer's two huge black dogs jumped out. In a minute they tore Tortoise to pieces.

So, in the end, Tortoise paid the price for his greed.

(c) Five minutes later, the farmer brought out a big sack and gave it to Tortoise. "Here's my boy in the sack. Please look after him."

Tortoise took the sack and hurried away. However, the sack was very heavy so he couldn't run very fast.

(d) "Oh, my goat, my beautiful goat," cried Tortoise. "Your son ate it in the night."

The farmer felt sorry for Tortoise. He offered Tortoise a cow to replace the goat.

D Comprehension 2

1 Did the farmer believe his son ate the goat?
2 Did the farmer give Tortoise his son?
3 What did the farmer put in the sack that he gave to Tortoise?
4 What happened to Tortoise?

Word focus 🔍

Make sentences with these words:

explain   invite   guess   replace   offer   greedy   rudely   tear to pieces

E Grammar

1 Look.

Use speech (or quotation) marks to show the words people say. The words inside the speech marks are a smaller sentence inside a bigger sentence. They start with a capital letter and end with a full stop, question mark or a exclamation mark. This is called **direct speech**.

Tortoise said, "I am cold and tired."

The spoken words can go first. In this case, a full stop is replaced by a comma (but question marks and exclamation marks do not change).

"I am cold and tired," said Tortoise.

2 Rewrite the following. Change the position of the spoken words.

(a) "You can leave it next to my son's bed," said the farmer.

The farmer said, "You can leave it next to my son's bed."

(b) Tortoise asked, "Can I have my hen, please?"

(c) "My hen, my beautiful hen!" cried Tortoise.

(d) Tortoise said rudely, "I don't want your cow. Give me your son."

3 Look at these verbs of speech. Can you add any more?

asked	answered	replied	explained	said
called	cried	shouted	screamed	whispered

Verbs of speech (**said, asked, answered**) tell us how a person speaks. Choose these verbs carefully and your writing will be more interesting.

4 Complete these sentences. Use correct punctuation and a verb of speech.

(a) Tortoise ... Can I have my goat now, please?

Tortoise asked, "Can I have my goat now, please?"

(b) The farmer ... Here's my son in this sack.

(c) That's very funny ... Chike.

(d) Be quiet, the baby is sleeping ... Mother.

(e) As the man fell out of the window, he ... Help me!

5 Look.

When we write about, or report, what someone says it is called **reported speech**. You do not need to use speech marks.

6 Complete the sentences of direct speech.

(a) Our teacher said we were making too much noise.

"You are _____ ," said our teacher.

(b) She told us to do our work.

"Do _____ ," she told us.

(c) The doctor told my mother to rest in bed.

The doctor said, "_____ "

(d) My mother said she was too busy.

"_____ ," she said.

F Speech

1 Tortoise is usually polite because it helps him to get what he wants. However, at the end he is greedy and rude to the farmer. Say these using the intonation shown.

May I stay the night with you?   I don't want your cow. Give me your son.

2 Say these with different intonation.

Not friendly or polite   **Friendly and polite**

Can I help you?   Can I help you?

Excuse me.   Excuse me.

3 Act out the story of 'Polite Tortoise'.

(a) Work in pairs to complete the table below.

A **scene** in a **drama** is where something happens. A **character** is a person or animal. The **action** is what happens.

Scene	Characters	Notes on the action
1 On the road	Tortoise and old woman	Pull out thorn. Tortoise gets an egg.
2 First village	Tortoise and man	Ask to stay. Put egg on plate. Eat egg in night. Tortoise gets a hen.
3 Second village		
4	Tortoise and farmer	
5 On the road	Tortoise and two dogs	

(b) Decide who will play each character.

(c) Decide the words to say and practise them.

(d) Rehearse the words and actions.

(e) Perform the drama.

G Dictation

Listen to your teacher. Write the paragraph.

> After the farmer's dogs had torn Tortoise to pieces, they went home. They arrived home an hour later. The farmer guessed what had happened but he didn't know for sure. He decided to report the incident to the police.

H Composition

Write a formal letter from the farmer to the police to report what happened. Include in your letter:

- an address for the farmer
- a date
- an address for the police station
- the opening 'Dear Sir or Madam'
- the title 'Missing Tortoise'
- the completed contents – see below (put the verbs in the correct tense)
- the closing 'Yours sincerely'
- a signature and a full name for the farmer.

I wish to report a serious incident. Last night Tortoise _____ (come) to my farm with a goat. He _____ (ask) to stay the night. I _____ (agree) and we _____ (leave) the goat with my son to look after.

In the morning the goat _____ (go). Its bones _____ (be) on my son's bed. I _____ (offer) Tortoise a cow to replace the goat. Tortoise rudely said he _____ (want) my son.

I _____ (know) it was a trick. I _____ (put) my two dogs in a sack and gave it to Tortoise. I _____ (tell) him it was my son so he left. An hour later the two dogs _____ (return).

I do not know what _____ (happen) to Tortoise. You might want to search for him.

7 A bicycle puncture

A Reading

Before reading: Have you ever repaired a bicycle puncture? What did you do?

Chike likes to play on his bicycle at the weekends. But today one of the bicycle tyres has a puncture. He's never repaired a puncture before and he doesn't know how to do it.

His sister, Joy, knows how to repair a puncture but she's too busy doing her homework.

Joy: I'll explain what you have to do and then you can do it.

Chike: OK, what do I do first?

Joy: First, you must find two tyre levers. Father has some in the kitchen cupboard. Then remove the tyre with the levers and pull out the inner tube. When you have done that, pump air into the inner tube with the bicycle pump.

Chike: Why? If there is a puncture won't the air just come out?

Joy: Yes, of course it will, but just listen to me, will you?

Chike: Sorry, go on.

Joy: Pump air into the inner tube and then quickly put the inner tube into a bucket of water. Air will escape from the tube and make bubbles in the water. You must find the bubbles to show you where the hole is. Once you have found the hole, take the tube out and mark the hole with a piece of chalk.

Chike: Right. Once I know where the hole is what do I do?

Joy: Dry the area around the hole and then stick a rubber patch over the hole. You will need some glue and a small rubber patch for that.

Chike: Where will I find them?

Joy: With the tyre levers in the kitchen cupboard.

Chike: OK, what next?

Joy: Put some glue around the hole and then press the patch down on top. Hold it tightly for a few minutes while the glue dries. Then put the inner tube back inside the tyre and fit the tyre back over the wheel using the tyre levers. Finally, pump up the tyre.

Chike: Umm. I think I understood all that but maybe I should write it all down so that I don't forget anything.

B Comprehension

1 When Chike tried to write it down he forgot some things. Use the pictures to make a list of *Things Needed* for Chike.

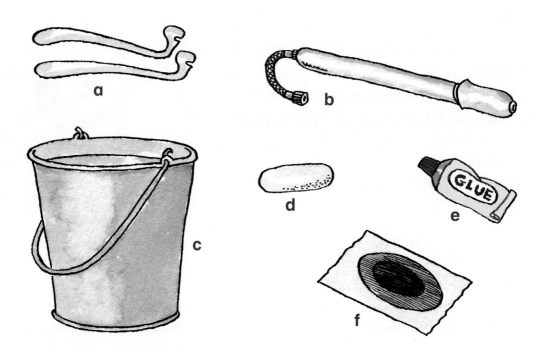

2 Copy and complete the *Things to do* list for Chike.

Remove the tyre with a tyre ___lever___ .

(a) Pull out the _____ and pump air into it.

(b) Put the inner tube into a _____ .

(c) Look at the tube carefully to find the _____ .

(d) Mark the hole with a piece of _____ .

(e) _____ the area around the puncture.

(f) Put some _____ around the hole and press down a rubber patch.

(g) Hold the _____ tightly while the glue dries.

(h) Put the inner tube back _____ the tyre and replace the tyre.

(i) _____ up the tyre.

3 Read the dialogue in pairs.

Word focus 🔍

Make sentences with these words:

puncture   repair   tyre   pump   bubble   hole   mark   glue

C Grammar

1 Look.

Study these examples of **direct** and **reported** speech:

Chike said, "My bicycle has a puncture."

Chike said his bicycle had a puncture.

Notice the changes we make when we are reporting what someone says:

- we do not use speech marks
- the verb tense changes (**has** to **had**)
- the pronouns change in some cases (**my** to **his**)

2 Put in the correct pronouns in the direct speech sentences.

(a) Chike said, "I need some glue."

Chike said _____ needed some glue.

(b) Joy said, "I will help Chike."

Joy said _____ would help Chike.

(c) Chike said, "Joy helped me."

Chike said Joy had helped _____ .

(d) Chike said, "We are finished."

Chike said _____ were finished.

(e) Joy said, "I didn't finish my homework."

Joy said _____ hadn't finished _____ homework.

(f) Mother said to Chike, "Your sister is very good to you."

Mother said to Chike _____ sister was very good to _____ .

3 Complete the sentences of reported speech.

(a) Aminat said, "The story is interesting."

Aminat said ...

(b) Usman said, "I don't like it."

Usman said ...

(c) Joy said, "I have to do my homework."

Joy said ...

(d) Chike said, "My bicycle is repaired."

Chike said ...

(e) "My teacher helps me," said Amina.

Amina said ...

(f) "I want to talk to your teacher," my father said.

My father said ...

D Speech

1 Name the parts of a bicycle.

wheel	tyre	pedal	handlebars	gears
brake	saddle	chain	bicycle pump	bell

2 Talk about either *My bicycle*, or *The bicycle I would like to have.*
- describe what it looks like (colour, size, number of gears, etc.)
- say what you like about it.

E Dictation

Listen to your teacher. Write the paragraph.

Chike found the tyre levers and all the other things he needed. It was difficult to get the tyre off the wheel but, after that, everything was easy. The hole was big so he quickly found where the air was escaping from. He repaired the puncture and was soon happily riding on his bike again.

F Composition

Imagine your bicycle has been stolen. Write a letter to the police to report the theft. Describe the bicycle. Say when it was stolen. Use the layout of a formal letter and formal language.

8 The invitation

A Reading 1

Before reading: Have you ever received an invitation card? What did it say?

Atinuke was happy. She walked into her classroom smiling. She pulled a bunch of envelopes from her bag. Aminat stared at her in surprise.

"Atinuke, why have you got so many letters?" she asked.

"They're not letters. They're invitation cards," explained Atinuke.

"Invitation cards for what?" Aminat wanted to know.

"For my birthday party!" said Atinuke with a wide grin.

"Really?" asked Aminat. "When is it?"

"A week on Saturday," Atinuke told her.

Atinuke walked around the class handing out invitation cards to her friends.

Aminat opened her envelope and looked at the card. It read:

> ## It's my birthday!
> ### Come and celebrate with me.
>
> To Miss Aminat Buhari
> You are invited to Atinuke Idowu's 10th birthday party
> On 14th December
> From 3.00 To 5.00pm
> At 39, Nyerere Road, Goldfield Estate
>
> *RSVP*
> *Bukola Idowu Tel. 354982*
> *Hope you can come!*

B Comprehension 1

1 Why does Atinuke have a lot of invitation cards?
2 Who does she give them to?
3 How old will Atinuke be on her birthday?
4 What date is the party?
5 What time is the party?
6 Where will the party be held?
7 Who do you think Bukola Idowu is?
8 Why is her telephone number on the invitation?

37

C Reading 2

Before reading: Do you invite everybody to your parties? Who do you invite?

When Atinuke handed Chike an envelope, Bala giggled and said, "I'd like to know what's in that."

Chike said, "It must be a letter of some sort."

"Or a secret message," joked Bala.

Chike tore open the envelope and quickly read the invitation. He was pleased that Atinuke had invited him to her party.

"Why hasn't she invited me?" Bala asked Chike.

"I don't know. Ask her," Chike said.

Bala pulled a silly face at Atinuke and asked, "Where is mine?"

"Your what?" asked Atinuke.

"My invitation to your party," said Bala.

Atinuke gave a big sigh. "Bala, I'm angry with you. I don't know if you are my friend or not!" she told him. "If you were my friend, you would have helped me when I fell over yesterday. Instead you stood and laughed at me!"

Bala took a deep breath and said, "You're right, that was bad of me. I'm sorry. Please forgive me."

"OK, that's better. Would you like to come to my birthday party?" asked Atinuke.

"Yes, please," replied Bala. "When is it?"

Atinuke said, "I'll write a card for you. I still have a spare one in my bag."

"Thanks, Atinuke," said Bala.

He waved the card at Chike, "Chike, look, I've got mine!"

D Comprehension 2

1 Did Atinuke give Chike an invitation?
2 Did she give Bala an invitation?
3 What did Chike tell Bala to do?
4 What did Bala ask for?
5 Why hadn't Atinuke invited Bala?
6 What had Bala done?
7 What did Bala do to make things better?
8 What did Atinuke do then?

E Grammar

1 Complete the sentences. Use **told** or **said**.

> **Told** and **said** are similar but when we use **told** we have to say **who** was spoken to.
>
> *Atinuke **said** it was a party invitation.*
> *Atinuke **told** Aminat the party was a week on Saturday.*

Chike ___said___ it must be a letter.

(a) Chike _____ Bala to ask Atinuke.

(b) Usman _____ his mother he would be late.

(c) Usman _____ he was going to play football.

(d) He _____ you he couldn't help.

(e) I _____ I couldn't help you.

(f) Mother asked me if I had _____ the teacher.

(g) Aminat _____ she liked parties.

2 Put the following into reported speech. They are all things Bala has been told or asked to do.

> To put a command into reported speech, use **told** or **asked**.
>
> *"Ask her," Chike said.*　　　*Chike **told** Bala to ask her.*
> *The teacher said, "Close the door*　*The teacher **asked** Bala to close*
> *please, Bala."*　　　　　　　　*the door.*

Don't be late for the party. 　　　 Be quiet, Bala.

(a) Atinuke asked Bala not to be late ...　　**(b)** The teacher ...

Please give an invitation to Musa. 　　Thank Atinuke for the invitation, please.

(c) Atinuke ...　　　　　　　　　　**(d)** Musa ...

Work hard at school.

Don't watch too much television.

(e) His father ...   **(f)** His mother ...

F Speech

1 Say these invitations politely. The intonation should rise at the end.
Would you like to come to my birthday party?
Would you like to come to my house?
Would you like to play with me?
Would you like to go shopping with us?

2 Say these responses.

> To sound polite, friendly and enthusiastic your voice must start high, fall and then rise.

Yes, please.   Wonderful.   Certainly.

3 Work in pairs. Take it in turns to give invitations and respond. Continue the conversations.
A: Would you like to come to my birthday party?
B: Yes, please. When is it?
A: Next Saturday.
B: Great. What time?
A: ...

G Dictation

Listen to your teacher. Write the paragraph.

> Atinuke's party will be a celebration of her birthday. We also have parties to celebrate other events. Families celebrate when babies are born, when couples get married and other important events. Students also celebrate when they pass exams.

H Composition

1 Write one of the dialogues that you had in Speech 3.
2 Write a birthday invitation card. Look at the card on page 37 as a guide.

9 Agriculture

A Reading 1

Before reading: What do you know about agriculture in Nigeria?

"Has he arrived yet?" asked Chike.

Usman looked out of the window. "Yes, he's here," he told his friend.

"How do you know?" Chike wanted to know.

"I can see a big car with 'Agricultural Department' written on the side," answered Usman.

At that moment the class teacher came in with the visitor.

"Good morning, Sir. Welcome to our class," greeted the pupils.

"Good morning, children," he replied.

"Children, this is Mr Fatope," said the teacher. "He's an Agricultural Officer. He is here to talk to us about agriculture in Nigeria."

Mr Fatope began, "Agriculture is very important for a country. Let's start at the beginning. Agriculture is the way we farm. The way we prepare the soil so that we can grow food on it and harvest it to eat or sell. It is also how we rear and manage animals."

Mr Fatope pointed to Aminat and asked, "Tell me how farmers prepare the soil, please?"

Aminat stood up and answered, "Sometimes they use hoes, cutlasses or their hands to prepare the soil. If it is a big farm they use ploughs with animals or tractors."

"Excellent!" said Mr Fatope.

B Comprehension 1

1 What is written on the visitor's car?

2 What is the visitor's name?

3 What is his job?

4 What does he talk to the class about?

5 Why do farmers prepare soil?

6 What are the two things we do with food we harvest?

7 What did Mr Fatope ask Aminat?

8 What ways of preparing the soil did Aminat mention for small farms?

41

C Reading 2

Before reading: What crops do farmers grow in Nigeria? And what animals do they keep?

"Good. I can see this class is very clever. There are three types of farming, arable, pastoral and mixed. Who can explain what they are?"

Usman jumped to his feet, "Arable farms grow crops. Pastoral farms keep animals and mixed farms keep animals as well as grow crops."

"Very good. Now, you ask me some questions," Mr Fatope told the class.

"What are some crops grown in Nigeria, sir?" asked Atinuke.

"There are many but some of them are cassava, maize, groundnuts, yams, beans and cocoa," he replied.

Atinuke put up her hand to ask a question, "Which animals are kept on pastoral farms?"

"We call animals on farms livestock. Again, there are many in Nigeria but perhaps the most common are cattle, goats and chickens," he explained. "Now, I have time for one more question."

"What are cash crops?" asked Bala.

"They are crops farmers grow to sell, not to eat themselves. For example, cocoa and cotton," said Mr Fatope.

D Comprehension 2

1 What are the three types of farming?
2 What do farmers do on mixed farms?
3 What are farm animals called?
4 Name the food crops in a to c, the livestock in d to f and the cash crops in g and h.

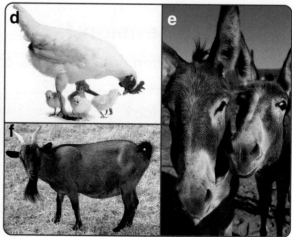

E Grammar

1 Look.

> To put a question into reported speech we often have to change the word order. The sentence is now a report, not a question.
>
> **Wh- questions**
>
> | | |
> |---|---|
> | *"Where is the visitor?"* | *Chike asked where the visitor was.* |
> | *"What are cash crops?"* | *Bala asked what cash crops were.* |
> | *"How are you?"* | *The visitor asked how I was.* |
>
> Note the changes when we report a question:
> * We do not use speech marks or a question mark.
> * The verb tense changes (it moves further into the past).
> * Pronouns may change.   • Word order may change.

2 Complete the reported speech.

(a) Mr Fatope asked, "What is agriculture?"

Mr Fatope asked what ...

(b) Usman asked, "Which animals do you like?"

Usman asked ...

(c) The policeman asked, "Where do you live?"

The policeman asked ...

(d) "Where do you go to school?" she asked.

She asked ...

(e) "What is Aminat doing?" she asked.

Atinuke asked ...

3 Report the questions.

> Use **if** when you put a **yes/no** question into reported speech.
>
> **Yes/no questions**
>
> "Has he arrived yet?"   Chike asked if he had arrived yet.
> "Do you understand?"   The teacher asked if we understood.

(a) *Chike:*   Usman, have you ever seen cocoa?
  Chike asked Usman if he had ...
(b) *Aminat:*   Bala, are you coming to my party?
  Aminat asked Bala ...
(c) *Atinuke:*   Mrs Buhari, is Aminat at home?
  Atinuke asked Mrs Buhari ...
(d) *Teacher:*   Chike, do you want help?
  The teacher asked ...
(e) *Teacher:*   Aminat, do you know the answer?
  The teacher ...
(f) *Mother:*   Usman, do you want a biscuit?
  Mother ...

F Speech

1 Copy and complete this word diagram. Add as many new words as you can.

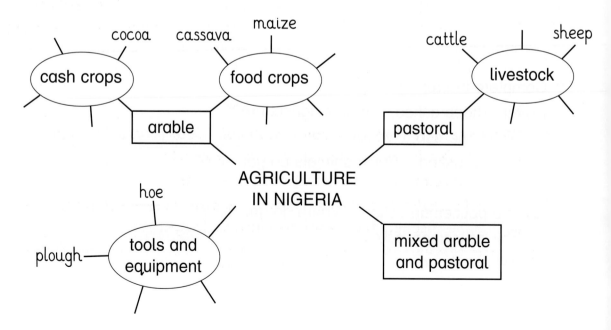

2 Give a two-minute talk on agriculture in Nigeria. You can use your word diagram to help you.

G Dictation

Listen to your teacher. Write the paragraph.

> Agriculture is a very old activity. The first men who lived collected leaves and plants, and hunted animals. They learnt which plants were best and started to grow them. They also captured animals to keep so that they could have enough to eat whenever they wanted. This was the beginning of farming.

H Composition

1 Write a short composition about agriculture in Nigeria. Use your word diagram and what you talked about in Speech above.

Remember, for each new topic or idea use a different paragraph. Use this outline:

Paragraph 1: Agriculture is very important because ... There are three types of farming, they are ...

Paragraph 2: Arable farming is ... Some food crops are ... Cash crops are ... Some Nigerian cash crops are ...

Paragraph 3: Pastoral farming is ... Some of the animals found on Nigerian farms are ...

2 Look at the invitation cards you wrote in Composition in Unit 8, page 40. Change your cards with a partner. Write a short letter to accept the invitation.

Fun box

Did you know ...

- ... there are more than 14 billion (14,000,000,000) farm animals in the world? This is twice as many as there are people.
- ... the most common vegetable crop is the potato?
- ... in the Seychelles islands the people grow palm trees which have huge double coconuts that weigh as much as 18kg?

10 Revision A

A Reading

Once the wind
Once the wind
said to the sea
I am sad
      And the sea said
Why
      And the wind said
Because I
am not blue like the sky
or like you

      So the sea said what's
so sad about that
          Lots
of things are blue
or red or other colours too
      but nothing
neither sea nor sky
can blow so strong
or sing so long as you

      And the sea looked sad
        So the wind said
Why

by Shake Keane

B Comprehension

1 Read the poem and answer.

  (a) Who is talking in the poem?

  (b) Why is the wind sad?

  (c) How does the sea try to make the wind happier?

  (d) What happens to the sea?

  (e) Why do you think the sea is sad?

2 The poem has no punctuation. Write it out as a story adding correct punctuation.

    Once the wind said to the sea, "I am sad." ...

3 Write it again. Use reported speech.

Once the wind told the sea he was sad. The sea asked why. ...

C Reading quiz

1 Find the answers in the reading texts in units 1–9.

(a) What colour is Adire cloth?

(b) Which part of a dictionary will show you the correct spelling of a word?

(c) Why didn't Atinuke go to Aminat's party?

(d) What was the heading in Mr Idowu's letter of 27 September?

(e) What was the wrong number that Atinuke dialled?

(f) What did the old woman pull out of Tortoise's foot?

(g) What was in the sack the farmer gave Tortoise?

(h) What do you use to remove a tyre from a bicycle wheel?

(i) What do you write on an invitation if you want someone to send a reply?

2 Write eight questions of your own about reading texts 1–9.

3 Ask your questions.

Word focus

Make sentences with these words:

celebrate   cough   definition   design   giggle   grin   infectious   joke
recover   remove   sigh   traditional

D Grammar

Read. Then copy the table and answer.

Some of the sentences below are correct. Some are incorrect.

- For each correct one you mark with a ✓ you get 1 point. For each incorrect one you mark with a ✗ you get 1 point.
- For each incorrect sentence you can make correct, you get 2 more points. Write the corrections in your exercise book.
- Be careful! If you write a sentence which is incorrect you lose a point.

	Correct	Incorrect	Points
This T-shirt was made by Aminat.	✓		1
The cloth is wash first.		✗	1
The cloth is washed first.			2

1 The cloth is put into the dye for five to eight minutes.

2 I like games who are played in teams.

3 At school we mustn't to eat during the lessons.

4 Children ought to help their parents at weekends.

5 I don't know what I'll do when I grow up. May I be a pilot.

6 You should to stay in the house when you have measles.

7 Usman asked, "Could you say that again, please?"

8 "Can I help," asked Chike.

9 Chike said his bicycle had a puncture.

10 Usman said Bala to ask Aminat.

11 Atinuke asked if the lesson interesting was.

12 My mother told me to do my homework.

E Speech

1 Say the following sentences politely.

  (a) Could you help me, please?

  (b) Would you like to come to my party?

  (c) Can I come in?

2 Work in pairs. Say the sentences above to each other. Continue the conversations.

3 Look at the pictures. Tell the story.

(a)   (b)   (c)

(d)   (e)   (f)

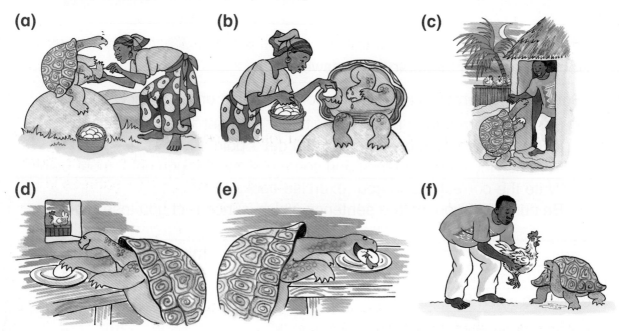

(g)   (h)   (i)

(j)   (k)   (l)

(m)   (n)   (o)

F Dictation

Look at the words in the Word focus box on page 43. Then listen to your teacher and write the dictation.

G Composition

1 Write the story of 'Polite Tortoise' you told in Speech above.

2 Imagine Mr Fatope came to your class last week to talk about agriculture in Nigeria. Write him a short formal letter to thank him. (His address is Agriculture Department, P.O. Box 57133, Lagos.)

Fun box

Can you answer this?

Mr and Mrs Esan have six daughters. Each daughter has one brother. How many people are there in the family?

11 Communication

A Reading

Before reading: How many ways of communicating do you know?

Writing letters

The first writing started about 3500 BC. It was used by a people called the Sumerians in the Middle East. About 5000 years ago, the Egyptians made pens and paper from reeds, a plant with long leaves that grows close to rivers. The first paper made from trees (as we use today) was produced in China in AD 105. Now millions of letters are written and sent every day.

Printing books, newspapers and magazines

Printing is a way of making many copies of text or a picture. Before the printing machines, books were copied one at a time, by hand. The Chinese made the first printing machine. However, they only became used a lot after 1454 when Johannes Gutenberg built his machine. Soon books, leaflets and newspapers were printed to spread information around the world. Modern printing machines produce hundreds of pages a second.

The telephone

When you send a letter to a friend, the friend reads it a few days later. With the telephone, someone hundreds of kilometres away can hear your message immediately. The telephone was invented in 1876. The latest telephones do not use wires. They use radio signals instead. This means people can take them out of their homes to use them at work, in the street or at the market. We call them mobile phones. They started in the mid-1980s.

Telegrams

Telegrams are a way of sending a written message quickly. The message is written by the sender and then sent by telegraph wire (like a telephone line). However, this form of communication is now out of date. It has been replaced by e-mail (see below) and communication from computer to computer.

Communicating with computers

The first computers were made in the 1940s. With a modern computer you can send e-mail. You can write a letter to a friend on a computer and then press a button to send it. There is no need for an envelope or a stamp! Your friend will receive the letter on his computer a few seconds later – even if it is the other side of the world.

There are now millions of computers around the world. The Internet has linked computers together since 1984. From a small computer in a home or school, you can communicate with many other computers. You can read newspapers and books and find all sorts of information.

B Comprehension 1

Are the following statements true or false?

1 The Egyptians invented writing. _false_
2 The paper we use today was invented by the Chinese. _true_
3 Before the printing press, books were copied by hand. _true_
4 The very first printing press was made by Johannes Gutenberg. _false_
5 A telephone allows immediate communication. _true_
6 Mobile phones use very small wires. _false_
7 Telegrams are still used a lot today. _false_
8 E-mail is an expensive way of communicating. _false_
9 E-mail is a very quick way of communicating. _true_
10 The Internet allows computer users to communicate with one another.
  true

C Comprehension 2

Complete.

Invention	Year
First writing	3500 BC
	3000 BC
Paper from wood	5,000
Gutenberg printing press	1454

Invention	Year
telephone	AD 1876
Computers	1940
mobile phones	mid-1980s
Internet	1984

Word focus 🔍

Make sentences with these words:

communication print copy text information invent mobile out of date

People text on a phone.

D Grammar _I get information from the internet._

1 Look.

Use **conjunctions** to join sentences and ideas in a text.

- Use **and** to join similar ideas.
  Millions of letters are written **and** sent every day.

- Use **but** to join opposing ideas.
  Telegrams were used a lot **but** are now out of date.

- Use **however** to start a new sentence with an opposing idea.
  Telegrams were used a lot. **However**, they are now out of date.

2 Write sentences with opposing ideas. Use **however**.

(a) The Chinese made the first printing machine.

   However, it was not widely used.

(b) Letters are a good way to communicate.

(c) There are now millions of computers around the world.

(d) Before printing machines, texts were copied one at a time.

3 Look.

- Use **although** (or **even though**) to join two ideas that seem to be opposed.
  *Atinuke wants a mobile phone, **although** she doesn't have much money.*
  Although can also start the sentence.
  ***Although** she doesn't have much money, Atinuke wants a mobile phone.*

4 Join the sentences twice. Use **although**.

(a) Telegrams are not used much now. They were used a lot.

   Telegrams are not used much now although they were used a lot.
   Although telegrams were used a lot, they are not used much now.

(b) Usman's mother telephones his grandmother every week. It costs a lot of money.

(c) Aminat is very thin. She eats a lot.

(d) The test was very difficult. Atinuke did well.

5 Look.

- Use **because** to explain the reason.
- Use **so** to give the result.
  *Telegrams are not used any more **because** e-mail is easier, quicker and cheaper.*
  *E-mail is easier, quicker and cheaper **so** telegrams are not used anymore.*

6 Complete the sentences twice. Use **because** and **so**.

(a) Usman's mother talked on the telephone for one hour ...

   because she had a lot to tell her mother.
   so it cost a lot of money.

(b) Atinuke wants to learn how to use the Internet ...

(c) Chike's mother bought some stamps ...

(d) Aminat got up early ...

E Speech

1 Say the sentences with correct intonation.

> For a list of items, use rising intonation on all items except the last.
> Use falling intonation on the last to show the list is finished.
>
> *Printing machines print books, magazines and newspapers.*

    (a) I use telephones, letters and e-mail.

    (b) The colours of the Ghanaian flag are red, yellow, green and black.

    (c) Would you like tea, coffee or a cool drink?

2 Play the game 'Just a minute' in groups of five.
You each have to speak for one minute about one of the topics in the box.

mobile phones	letters	telegrams	computers	e-mail
television	magazines	conversation	newspapers	radio

    (a) The speaker must *not*

       hesitate ("um ... er ..."); deviate from the subject (talk about anything else); repeat anything (say the same thing more than once).

    (b) The others in the group can challenge the speaker if they hear hesitation, deviation or repetition. If the judge agrees with them, the challenger carries on speaking about the topic for the rest of the minute.

    (c) One of you must be the judge. Your job is to

       time the speech; decide if challenges are correct or not; give points (one point for a correct challenge, two points for speaking at the end of the minute).

F Dictation

Listen to your teacher. Write the paragraph.

> Telegrams were always short because people had to pay for each word. They only used the most important words. For example, if they wanted to invite someone to a wedding the telegram might be, NKECHI MARRIES JANUARY 12 COME.

G Composition

Work in pairs and act out a telephone conversation. Talk about either your family or what you did in the holidays.

Then work together to write out your telephone conversation.

12 The farmer, his son and the donkey

A Reading 1

Before reading: Look at the picture. What do you think is happening? Why are the men shouting at the boy?

While a farmer and his son were taking their donkey to market, they passed a group of boys on the way to school. The schoolboys laughed at the man and boy because they were walking. "You fools," one said. "Why don't you ride that donkey?"

The farmer did not like people laughing at him. He quickly put his son on the donkey and hurried on through the village. As they passed a compound some men saw the boy on the donkey and said, "There, look at that! The young boy sits and rests while the old man walks. There is no respect for the old! You wicked child, get down off that donkey and let your father ride."

The son did not want people to think he was disrespectful so he jumped down and helped his father up onto the donkey's back. The three walked on. A short while later, they passed a group of women and children working in the fields. The women were angry to see the man sitting comfortably and his son walking in the heat and dust. They shouted at the farmer, "There, that's a man for you. He sits there like a chief while his own son suffers."

B Comprehension 1

1 Where were the farmer and his son going?
2 Where were the boys going?
3 Why did the boys laugh at the farmer and his son?
4 What did the farmer do as a result of the schoolboys' laughter?
5 Why were the men angry with the farmer's son?
6 What did the boy do as a result of what the men said?
7 Why did the women shout at the farmer?
8 What do you think the farmer did as a result of the women's shouts?

C Reading 2

Before reading: How do you think the story will end?

As soon as he heard the women, the farmer pulled the boy up to sit in front of him on the donkey. They continued like this until they arrived at the market town. Everyone looked at them as they passed. The farmer stopped the donkey and asked a woman why everyone was staring. The woman answered, "Well, we're surprised by the way you treat your donkey. You're going to break its back! Then you won't be able to sell it at the market."

So father and son climbed down. They thought and they thought about what they could do. At last they had an idea. They cut down a thick branch from a tree and tied the donkey's feet to it. Then they lifted the branch and the donkey to their shoulders and carried it.

Now everyone shouted and laughed. The donkey was frightened by the noise. It tried to break free as they were crossing a bridge. The men dropped the branch and the donkey fell off the bridge into the river. Its feet were still tied to the branch so it could not swim. It quickly drowned.

The farmer and his son went home sadly. When they told their story, a wise man told them to think carefully about their adventure and to learn a lesson from it.

D Comprehension 2

1 In each of the first five paragraphs the farmer, his son and the donkey are **walking** or **being carried**. Complete this table and say what the three of them are doing in each paragraph.

Paragraph	Farmer	Son	Donkey
1	walking	walking	walking
2		being carried	
3			
4			
5			

2 What happened to the donkey?

3 What did the farmer and his son do then?

4 What is the lesson of the story the wise man talked about? Is it

  (a) Many hands make light work.

  (b) Try to please all and you will please none.

  (c) A stitch in time saves nine.

Word focus 🔍

Make sentences with these words:

hurry   wicked   disrespectful   comfortably   suffer   treat   branch
adventure

E Grammar

1 Look.

Some **conjunctions** tell us about time or the order of events.

- **before/after**

  After the schoolboys laughed at him, the farmer put his son on the donkey.
  Before the women shouted at them, the farmer was riding the donkey.

- **when/as soon as**

  The donkey fell off the bridge **when** they dropped it.
  As soon as he heard the women, the farmer put the boy in front of him on the donkey.

- **while/as**

  While they were walking through the streets, people were laughing at them.
  They were carrying the donkey **as** they crossed the bridge.

- **until**

  The farmer and his son did not ride the donkey **until** the schoolboys laughed at them.

2 Choose the correct conjunction.

  (a) The wise man told the farmer and his son to learn the lesson from their adventure *when/before* they told him what happened.

  (b) The farmer and his son didn't carry the donkey *when/until* the woman said they were going to break its back.

  (c) The phone rang *as/after* I was leaving the house.

  (d) Usman arrived at home *while/until* Aminat was talking on the phone.

  (e) I'll help you *as/as soon as* I finish my work.

3 Complete these sentences.

    (a) The boy got off the donkey when ...

    (b) I hurt my leg while ...

    (c) Atinuke did not understand the lesson until ...

    (d) I think I lost my money as ...

    (e) I did my homework after ...

    (f) I did my homework as soon as ...

    (g) I did my homework before ...

F Speech

1 Put the pictures into the correct order.

(a)   **(b)**

            (c)   **(d)**

(e)   **(f)**

2 Retell the story.

G Dictation

Listen to your teacher. Write the paragraph.

> 'Try to please all and you will please none' is a proverb. A proverb is an old and popular saying which contains traditional wisdom. Very often proverbs give advice. 'Many hands make light work' and 'a stitch in time saves nine' are also proverbs.

H Composition

Complete the story in your own words.

A farmer and his son were taking a donkey to market when …
The schoolboys …
The farmer …
While they were passing a compound, …
The boy …
As they were passing a field …
When he heard this, the farmer …
The two of them rode the donkey until …
They got off and …
They decided to …
They carried it across …
When the donkey heard people laughing it …
It drowned because …
The lesson of this story is …

13 Congratulations!

A Reading 1

Before reading: When do people have celebrations?

Atinuke's mother has two parties to attend in one week. She drew a circle around the date of her brother's wedding on the calendar. She also circled the date for Mrs Aregbesola's baby's naming ceremony. She planned to buy cards and gifts to take to the ceremonies.

"Remember to send your friend our congratulations on the birth of her baby," said Atinuke's father.

"I'm going to buy a card and a present for the baby. I also have to get a card and a present for my brother," she answered.

"What's 'congratulations'?" asked Tunji, Atinuke's young brother.

"It's our way of saying that we are happy for them," explained his mum.

"Mummy, when are you going to buy the cards and presents?" asked Atinuke.

"Maybe tomorrow," replied her mother.

Atinuke asked, "Can I go? I want to go with you."

"Why?" her mother wanted to know.

"I have to buy a card and a present for Hairat. It is her tenth birthday next week. I showed you my invitation card, didn't I?" said Atinuke.

"Yes, I saw it," replied her mum.

B Comprehension 1

1 What two parties is Atinuke's mother going to attend?

2 Where did Atinuke's mother mark the dates of the ceremonies?

3 What did she want to buy?

4 What does it mean if we say 'Congratulations' to someone?

60

5 When is Atinuke's mother going shopping?

6 Where did Atinuke want to go?

7 Why did Atinuke want to go shopping?

8 What celebration is Hairat holding next week?

C Reading 2

Before reading: Have you been to a wedding or naming ceremony? What happened?

At the shop, there were many congratulation cards and gifts. They were for weddings, the birth of new babies, housewarmings, graduations and many more. Atinuke and her mum looked through the cards to find suitable ones.

"I like this one! I'll get it for my brother," said her mum.

"Let's see," Atinuke said as she took it from her mum.

"The picture is beautiful." She read the front – *Congratulations on your Wedding!* Then, she opened it -

Celebrate and enjoy your special day!

Marriage is a gift to give each other
A present of love and tender care.
Now starts a new life together
Which is only yours to share.

We wish you much love and happiness.

"Let's buy it. I like the message in it," said Atinuke's mum.

They also bought cards and gifts for Mrs Aregbesola and Hairat.

On the day of the naming ceremony, Atinuke, her brother, and her parents drove to Mrs Aregbesola's house. Mrs Aregbesola met them at the door.

"Congratulations!" said Atinuke's parents to her.

"Thanks," she smiled.

"That's for the baby," Atinuke's mum gave her the card and the gift.

"Thanks for the gift and for coming," replied Mrs Aregbesola.

They had a look at the baby and then they sat down to enjoy the party with the others.

D Comprehension 2

1 What did Atinuke and her mother look at in the shop?

2 What is a housewarming?

3 What is a graduation?

4 What was the message on the front of the card Atinuke's mother chose for her brother?

5 What else did Atinuke and her mother buy?

6 Where was the naming ceremony held?

7 What did Atinuke's mother and father say to Mrs Aregbesola?

8 What did Mrs Aregbesola reply?

Word focus 🔍

Make sentences with these words:

circle   congratulations   plan   gift   suitable   ceremony

E Grammar

1 Look.

To describe actions that started in the past and continue up to now, use the **present perfect continuous** tense.

$$\begin{matrix} \textbf{have} \\ \textbf{has} \end{matrix} + \textbf{been} + \text{present participle (verb + \textbf{ing})}$$

Atinuke has been looking for cards and gifts.
I have been learning English for six years.

2 Make sentences from the table.

I You We They	have		living in this town all my life.
			sitting in the classroom all morning.
			working hard this week.
		been	listening to the teacher all lesson.
He She It	has		watching what is happening outside.
			learning English for ... years.
			studying at this school for ... years.

3 Make sentences about what has been happening.

62   (a) Usman has been walking in the rain.

(b) (c) (d) (e)

(f) (g) (h) (i)

F Speech

1 Say the following.

> When you congratulate someone you must sound happy and enthusiastic.
> To show enthusiasm, the voice must start high, fall and then rise again.

Congratulations!   Happy birthday!   Well done!   Excellent!

2 Work in pairs. Act out the conversation.

B has a new baby. A is arriving for a naming ceremony.

A: Congratulations!

B: Thanks.

A: Here's a gift for the baby.

B: Thank you. And thank you for coming. Please come in and see the baby.

A: Thank you. Oh! What a beautiful baby!

3 Work in pairs and act out the conversations. One of you is A. The other is B.

(a) It is A's birthday. B is a good friend.

(b) B is getting married. A is an old friend.

(c) A has a new house. B is arriving for the housewarming party.

(d) B has passed his/her exams. A is a teacher.

G Dictation

Listen to your teacher. Write the paragraph.

> The day after the naming ceremony, Atinuke and her family attended the wedding. It was very exciting. Atinuke loved to see her uncle in his smart suit and her new aunt in her long white dress. There was lots of food and many other children to play with. All the children shouted 'congratulations!' when the couple left the party.

H Composition

1 Write a letter to a friend who lives in another part of Nigeria. It is your friend's birthday.

2 Write a letter to an uncle who has just passed his exam to finish university. This should be a formal letter.

You can use some of the following phrases:

- Please accept my congratulations on your exam success.
- It was a brilliant achievement.
- I hope one day I will be able to repeat your success.

Fun box

Answer these riddles.

- What is the difference between here and there?
- What gets bigger when you take more away?
- What do you see less of the more there is of it?
- What gets wetter the more it dries?

14 Food and drink

A Reading and comprehension 1

Before reading: What is your favourite food? Do you know how to cook it?

Pepper Soup

INGREDIENTS [For 4–6 people]

1kg beef or goat   water
6 big fresh tomatoes   salt (to taste)
1 medium-sized onion   any other vegetable (optional)
I dried red pepper (or more, to taste)

METHOD

1

2

3

4

5

6

7

8

Put the instructions in the correct order. Use the pictures to help.

(a) Chop onions, tomatoes and pepper.

(b) Cook the meat in boiling water.

(c) Wash, clean, chop and add any other vegetables.

(d) Wash and cut meat into small pieces.

(e) Add chopped onions, tomatoes and peppers to meat and stir.

(f) Eat with rice or boiled yam.

(g) Add enough water to cover and leave on a low heat.

(h) Leave to simmer until meat is tender. Stir from time to time to prevent burning.

B Reading 2

Before reading: Look at the picture. What do you think the story is about?

Once upon a time, a chief called his people to a feast. He invited them all but told them that each man should bring one bottle of palm wine.

The day of the feast came. The adults put on their best clothes and walked to the chief's house with their families. They stopped at the door of the chief's house and poured the contents of their bottles into a very big pot at the door.

Mubo wanted to attend with all his friends but he had no palm wine at home. His wife said to him, "You must buy some palm wine."

Mubo answered, "What? No, I'm not going to buy wine for a feast that is free."

He thought a little and then said, "Hundreds of people will bring their wine and pour it into the pot. One bottle of water will not be noticed in so much palm wine."

So he went to the feast with a bottle of water. He poured his bottle into the pot as other people did. Then he sat down with all the others and waited for the glass of palm wine which he liked so much.

The chief said, "Let us drink wine!"

All the guests lifted their glasses to their lips eagerly and began to drink. However, they all stopped drinking as quickly as they had started. What they were drinking was not palm wine, but – water!

You see, everyone had thought the same thing, "One bottle of water will not be noticed in so much palm wine."

C Comprehension 2

1 What did the chief want every man to bring to the feast?

2 What did Mubo's wife want him to do?

3 Why didn't he want to buy any palm wine?

4 What did Mubo take to the feast?

5 What did he do with his water?

6 What did the men want to drink?

7 What did they drink?

8 What had they all thought?

Make sentences with these words:

optional chop stir simmer tender cover prevent
feast pour contents notice eagerly

D Grammar

1 Look.

> To describe an action that started in the past and is still continuing, use the **present perfect continuous** tense.
> *I have been cleaning the bathroom.*
>
> If the action is *finished* then we use the **present perfect** tense.
> *I have cleaned the bedroom.*

2 Read and answer.

The Buhari family are having a clean up at home. Atinuke is helping Aminat. Look at the jobs they have to do. Which ones have they done? Which haven't they done?

Mrs Buhari:
clean the Kitchen
• wash the dishes ✓
• clean the windows ✗

Mr Buhari: clean the outside of the house
• paint the walls ✓
• repair the door ✗

Aminat and Atinuke: clean the bedrooms
• sweep the floors ✓
• clean the windows ✗

Usman: tidy up
• pick up the toys ✓
• put away the clothes ✗

At lunchtime they all stop for a rest. What do they say?

I have been cleaning the kitchen. I have washed the dishes but I haven't cleaned the windows yet.

I _____ the outside of the house. I _____ the walls but I _____ the door yet.

We _____
_____
_____
_____

I _____
_____
_____
_____

3 Complete the sentences.

(a) Mrs Buhari has been _____ the kitchen. She _____ the dishes but she _____ the windows yet.

(b) Mr Buhari has been ...

(c) Aminat and Atinuke have been ...

(d) Usman ...

E Speech

1 Say the sentences with correct intonation.

When we offer a choice using *or*, we use rising intonation on the first choice and falling intonation on the second.

Do you want rice or boiled yam with the pepper soup?

(a) Do you prefer water or palm wine?

(b) Would you like tea or coffee?

(c) Do you want a blue or green one?

2 Work in pairs. Take it in turns to give instructions on how to do the following:

- prepare vegetables for cooking
- wash and clean pots and pans
- clean teeth
- polish shoes
- wash clothes

F Dictation

Listen to your teacher. Write the instructions to cook rice.

1 Rinse rice (optional).
2 Put rice, water, salt, and cooking oil or margarine in pan.
3 Bring to the boil; stir once or twice.
4 Cover with lid and simmer for twenty minutes.
5 Eat with stew or soup.

G Composition

Write a recipe for one of your favourite foods.

- Make a list of ingredients – the things you need.
- Write the method – a list of instructions of what to do. Use numbers to show the order of the instructions.
- Draw some pictures to help explain your instructions, if you want.

15 The three brothers

A Reading 1

Before reading: Look at the picture. What do you think the story is about?

Once upon a time, there were three brothers who loved the same girl. First Aziz, then Bamidele and finally Kabo went to the house of the girl and asked her the same question, "Fatimah, will you marry me?"

Fatimah didn't know what to do. She liked each of the three young men very much and could not decide which of them was the best. All of them were clever, handsome, strong and kind.

One day Fatimah's father had an idea. He said to the three brothers, "You must go on a long journey to find a gift for my daughter. It must be something useful. If she accepts it, it will be her dowry."

The three brothers travelled far and wide and they each bought a gift for the girl.

Aziz bought a magic carpet. He said, "This carpet can be used to fly anywhere in the world."

Bamidele bought a magic mirror. He said, "This mirror can be used to see anywhere in the world. When I look into my mirror, I can see anyone and everything that I want to see."

Kabo bought a magic lemon. He said, "The juice of my lemon can be used to make a dying man or woman well again."

B Comprehension 1

1 What did the three brothers want?
2 Which of the three brothers did she want to marry?
3 What was Fatimah's father's idea?
4 (a) What did Aziz buy?   (b) What is it used for?
5 (a) What did Bamidele buy?   (b) What is it used for?
6 (a) What did Kabo buy?   (b) What is it used for?

C Reading 2

Before reading: What do you think the three brothers will do with their presents? Who do you think Fatimah will marry?

Kabo said to his brothers, "We are far from our home and from our dear girl. Let's look into the mirror and see her."

So Bamidele took out his mirror and they all looked into it. They saw that Fatimah was very ill. Aziz quickly ordered his brothers to sit down on his carpet, and away they flew. They were at Fatimah's house in no time. Kabo cut and squeezed his magic lemon and gave the juice to Fatimah. She drank it, and was soon well again.

The young men were very happy. "Now which of us will you marry?" they asked Fatimah.

"I thank you all, my dear friends," answered Fatimah. "Bamidele saw me in his mirror and that helped to save my life. It is a very useful thing and he will have it for as long as he lives."

"Aziz used his carpet to bring you here and that helped to save me, too. It is also a very useful thing and he will have it for as long as he lives."

"However, Kabo used his lemon to make me well again. He gave all he had to save me – now he has nothing. That is the best dowry. I will be his wife."

D Comprehension 2

1 What did the brothers see when they looked in the mirror?
2 What did Aziz do when he saw Fatimah was ill?
3 What did Kabo do when they arrived at Fatimah's house?
4 What happened to Fatimah?
5 Who did she choose to marry?
6 Why did she choose him?

Word focus 🔍

Make sentences with these words:
handsome   useful   accept   dowry   far and wide   lemon juice   squeeze

E Grammar

1 Look.

> There are several ways to describe the function of an object.
>
> *The magic mirror is used to see Fatimah at home.*
> *The brothers use the magic mirror to see Fatimah at home.*
> *The brothers see Fatimah, using the magic mirror.*

2 Write three sentences about each of the following. Use the sentences above as examples.

  (a) the magic carpet   **(b)** the magic lemon   **(c)** a recipe

  (d) a mobile phone   **(e)** an e-mail

3 Look.

> Use **as … as** to say that two things are the same in some way.
>
> *Aziz is **as** tall **as** Bamidele.*
> *Aziz will have his carpet **as** long **as** he lives.*
>
> Use **not as … as** to say that two things are different in some way.
>
> *Kabo is **not as** old **as** Bamidele.*
> *Some gifts are **not as** useful **as** others.*

4 Write sentences. Use **(not) as … as**.

  (a) Kabo is younger than Aziz.   Kabo is not as old as Aziz.

  (b) Zube and Hairat are the same height.   Zube …

  (c) My bike is faster than yours.   Your bike …

  (d) Our team played better than theirs.   Their team …

  (e) Both Aziz and Kabo are equally kind.   Aziz is as …

  (f) Our new car is smaller than the old one.   Our new car …

5 Look.

> Use **the same … as** to make comparisons as well.
>
> *Aziz is **the same** height **as** Bamidele.*
> *My dress is **the same** colour **as** yours.*

6 Compare yourself to some other pupils in your class. Write ten sentences.

> I'm as old as Aishat. I'm not as tall as her. I have the same uniform as her.

F Speech

1 Work in groups. Think of as many uses as you can for each object below. They do not have to be serious uses. One of the group should write a sentence for each use. The group with the most uses wins.

A hoe	can could might	be used	for hoeing. for getting balls off a roof. for reaching under cupboards.

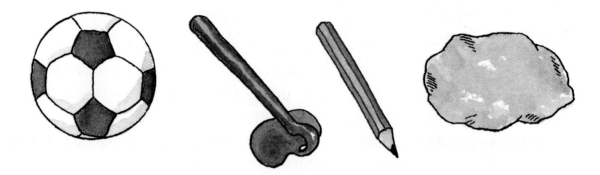

2 Work in groups. Think of as many comparisons as you can between the objects above. One of the group should write a sentence for each comparison. The group with the most correct sentences wins.

Use **not as ... as**.

The stone is not as big as the ball.
The pencil is not as hard as the stone.
The stone is not as useful as the hoe.

G Dictation

Listen to your teacher. Write the paragraph.

> Aziz and Bamidele were sad to hear Fatimah's decision but they understood it. They knew it was fair so they accepted it. They immediately began to help the young couple and Fatimah's father to organise the wedding. It was to be a huge ceremony with five hundred guests.

H Composition

1 Imagine you are Fatimah or Kabo. Write a letter to a friend to tell your friend about who you are marrying and how you decided to get married.

2 Imagine you are Fatimah or Kabo. Write a formal invitation card to your wedding.

16 The earrings

A Reading 1

Before reading: Do you ever argue with your brothers or sisters? What about?

Usman watched as Aminat opened the little blue jewellery box. Rays of sun from the high windows fell on Aminat's new pair of earrings in the box. They sparkled as the sun shone on them.

"Wow! They shine like diamonds," Usman said.

"Yes, I know. That's why I like them so much," replied Aminat.

"Have you written to Grandma to thank her for them?" asked Usman.

"Of course, that was the first thing I did as soon as I received them," answered Aminat.

"Good. Now that you have new earrings, I hope you won't want to borrow the watch she gave me for my birthday," Usman said.

"I still want to wear it sometimes," said Aminat.

"No, it doesn't belong to you, it's mine!" said Usman angrily.

"You're my brother and what's yours is mine!" replied his sister.

Usman was furious now, "No, if you use my watch again, I'll take your earrings!"

Aminat laughed, "Take them for what? Boys don't wear earrings like this."

She walked out of the room angrily.

The next day, Aminat did borrow Usman's watch. She wanted to wear it when she went to visit Atinuke. However, she was afraid Usman might find out and take her earrings so she decided to hide them.

B Comprehension 1

1 What did Usman watch Aminat do?

2 Why did the earrings sparkle?

3 Who gave Aminat the earrings?

4 What did Grandma give Usman?

5 What did Aminat want to borrow?

6 Did Usman want her to borrow the watch?

7 Did Aminat borrow the watch again?

8 Why did she want to hide her earrings?

C Reading 2

Before reading: Where will Aminat hide the earrings? What will happen?

Aminat thought for a moment about where to hide her earrings. She decided to put them on top of their parents' tall wardrobe. However, she was too short to reach the top so she had to stand on a chair. She pulled an old brown chair from the sitting room and climbed onto it.

She could now just reach the top if she stood on her tiptoes. She stretched to put the earrings out of sight. As she did this, the chair wobbled and she fell like a ton of bricks onto the floor. She cried out in pain. She had twisted her ankle.

No one heard her. She couldn't walk so she sat there and cried a little. She was sad because she knew that this was all her fault.

She talked to herself sadly, "I caused this pain for myself because I took Usman's watch. As a result I had to hide my earrings on top of the wardrobe. I needed a chair so that I could reach the top which is why I fell down and hurt my ankle. Why did I take the watch in the first place after Usman told me not to?"

D Comprehension 2

1 Where did Aminat decide to hide the earrings?
2 Why did she need a chair?
3 Could she reach the top of the wardrobe easily when she stood on the chair?
4 What happened to the chair?
5 What happened to Aminat?
6 Was she hurt?
7 Whose fault was the accident?
8 What did Aminat do wrong?

Word focus 🔍

Make sentences with these words:

argue   jewellery   ray   furious   tiptoes   wobble
like a ton of bricks   twist   ankle   pain   fault

E Grammar

1 Look.

> Use **so**, **therefore**, **as a result** to explain the results, or consequences, of something.
> - **So** is the most common. **Therefore** is more formal. They are usually used to join two sentences.
> - **As a result** is more formal and starts a new sentence.
>
> | | |
> |---|---|
> | *Aminat took Usman's watch,* | ***therefore** she had to hide her earrings.* |
> | *Aminat fell off the chair.* | ***As a result** she hurt herself.* |
> | *Aminat twisted her ankle* | ***so** she couldn't walk.* |

2 Complete the sentences.

(a) Aminat wanted to hide her earrings, therefore ...

(b) She decided to hide her earrings on top of the wardrobe so ...

(c) Aminat needed to be taller, therefore ...

(d) The chair wobbled. As a result ...

(e) Aminat took Usman's watch. As a result ...

3 Look.

> Use **so ... that** or **such ... that** to talk about results.
> - Use **so ... that** with an adjective (but no noun) or an adverb.
> - Use **such ... that** with (adjective +) a noun.
>
> *The wardrobe was **so** high **that** Aminat needed a chair to reach the top.*
> *It was **such** a wobbly chair **that** Aminat fell off it.*

4 Complete the sentences. Use **so** or **such**.

It was ___such___ a high wardrobe that Aminat could not reach the top.

(a) Aminat stretched _____ far that she fell off the chair.

(b) It was _____ an old chair that it wobbled.

(c) Aminat fell _____ heavily that she twisted her ankle.

(d) She twisted her ankle _____ badly that she couldn't walk.

(e) Aminat had _____ a bad fall that she cried.

5 Complete these sentences in your own words.

(a) It was such a hot day that ...

(b) The food was so bad that ...

(c) It was such a good story that ...

(d) I ate so much that ...

75

F Speech

1 Say the following.

> Rising intonation sounds more polite. You can change from a command (or order) to a polite request or offer with a change of intonation.
>
> Sit down.   Sit down?

Ring the bell.   Ring the bell?

Hurry up!   Hurry up, please.

Don't go away.   Don't go away, will you?

2 Hold a class debate on the motion:

Children should be free to wear what they want (for example, boys should be free to wear earrings and girls should be free to wear trousers).

(a) Work in groups. Prepare all your ideas for the topic.

(b) Listen to your teacher explain how to organise the debate.

- *Proposers:* prepare a speech to propose the motion. Think of all the ideas you can to support it.
- *Opposers:* prepare a speech to oppose the motion. Think of all the ideas you can against it.
- *Rest of class:* think of questions to ask the speakers.

G Dictation

Listen to your teacher. Write the paragraph.

> Usman looked at his watch for the tenth time in a minute. He admired its shiny red face and the sparkling silver hands and numbers. He pulled again on the black leather strap to make sure it was not going to fall off.
>
> "Chike," he asked, "do you want to know the time?"

H Composition

1 Write the letter from Aminat to her grandmother to thank her for the earrings.

2 Read again the description of Aminat's earrings in the first paragraph of the story on page 73 and the description of Usman's watch in Dictation above. Write a paragraph to describe a gift you have received.

17 A new apartment

A Reading 1

Before reading: Copy and complete the word diagram.

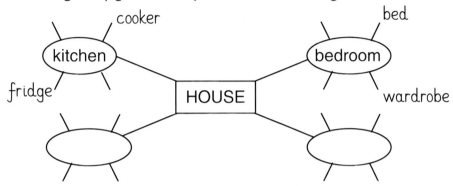

The Faleti family are moving into a new apartment. Mr and Mrs Faleti, Bunmi and Lola are deciding where to put their furniture.

The Faleti family furniture		
• Lola's bed	• Wardrobe	• Sofa
• Bunmi's bed	• Mirror	• Armchair
• Double bed	• Fridge	• Dining table and chairs
• Bedside tables	• Cooker	• Small table
• Cupboard	• Kitchen table	• Bookcase

Mr Faleti: Well, where does everything go? I don't know where to start.

Mrs Faleti: Let's start where it is easy. The small bedroom will be for the girls and there is only space to put their two beds next to one another.

Bunmi: I want the one next to the window.

Lola: OK, then mine will be nearest to the door.

Mrs Faleti: Good, that's agreed. And then there is just the cupboard for the clothes that will go at the end of the beds, next to the door.

Mr Faleti: Then in our bedroom, our double bed will also go against the wall opposite the door.

Mrs Faleti: Yes. It can go in the middle of the wall so that there will be room for the bedside tables on each side of the bed.

Mr Faleti: Then the wardrobe can go at the end of the bed next to the door and the mirror in the corner.

Lola: Is that all? Can we go and visit the new neighbours now?

B Comprehension 1

1 Why are the Faleti family talking about where to put their furniture?
2 How many different items of furniture have they got?
3 How many beds have they got?
4 Which room do they start in?
5 Whose bed will go nearest to the door?
6 Where will the girls' clothes cupboard go?
7 Where will the parents' bedside tables go?
8 Where will the mirror go?

C Reading 2

Before reading: In which rooms do you think the rest of the furniture will go?

Mrs Faleti:	Not just yet. Help us with the other rooms first. Let's decide on where things will go in the kitchen next.
Mr Faleti:	OK, let's put the fridge at the far end from the door, next to the sink.
Mrs Faleti:	No, I don't think so. I want the cooker there. And if we put the kitchen table next to it, opposite the sink, then we can do all the cooking in that area.
Bunmi:	But what about the fridge?
Mr Faleti:	That can go between the door and the table.
Mrs Faleti:	Yes, that's fine. Now what about the living room?
Mr Faleti:	The dining table is round so I think it will be better if we put it in the middle of the room. With the chairs, of course.
Mrs Faleti:	Yes, I agree. Then I think we can put the sofa and armchair at the end of the room near the big window.
Lola:	Are you going to put them right next to each other?
Mr Faleti:	No, I don't think so. Let's put the small table between them.
Mrs Faleti:	Good. But let's have the old armchair against the kitchen wall and the sofa on the other side because there's more room there.
Mr Faleti:	Fine, and then we'll have to put the bookcase at the other end of the room, up against our bedroom wall.
Mrs Faleti:	It'll look good there. So that's it – we're all agreed. OK, you can go outside now, girls. Thanks for your help.

Word focus 🔍

Make sentences with these words:

at the end of   at the far end   at the other end
opposite   each side of   in the corner

D Comprehension 2

Look at the plan of the Faleti's new apartment. Match the furniture to the letters on the plan.

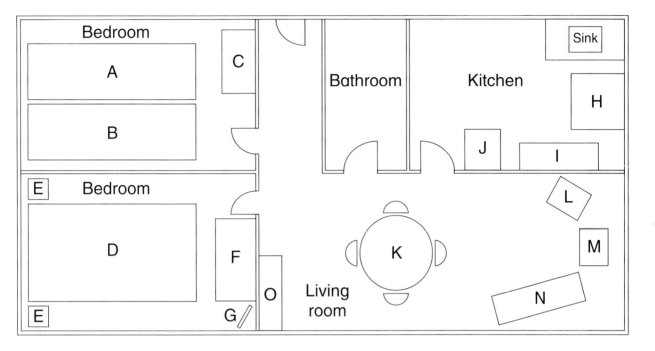

E Grammar

1 Ask and answer questions about the picture on the next page. Use words from the box.

Where is the dining table?   It's in the corner of the room.

| in   on   behind   in front of   opposite   between   next to   against |
| in the middle   around   above   below   on each side of   in the corner of |

2 Complete the sentences with words from the box in 1.

The table is _in the corner of_ the room.

(a) The bowl is _____ the table.

(b) The fruit is _____ the bowl.

(c) The light is _____ the table.

(d) The table is _____ the light.

(e) The dining chairs are _____ the table.

(f) The blue armchair is _____ the small table.

(g) The small table is _____ the two armchairs.

(h) The two armchairs are _____ the small table.

(i) The armchairs and small table are _____ the wall.

(j) The TV is _____ of the room.

(k) Chike is _____ the TV.

(l) Usman is _____ the curtain.

(m) Atinuke and Aminat are _____ each other.

3 Draw a simple plan of your bedroom. Write ten sentences about where the furniture is.

F Speech

1 Work in pairs. Show the plan of your bedroom you made in Grammar 3 on page 80. Describe your bedroom to your partner.

2 Follow these instructions.

(a) Take a clean piece of paper. On the top right corner of the paper write **A**.

(b) Turn the paper over and on the top left corner write **B**.

(c) On side A draw a large rectangle, just a little bit smaller than the paper. This is the plan of a room.

(d) In your rectangle draw five pieces of furniture. You can draw anything that you want but don't let anyone else see what you draw.

(e) Turn over to side B and draw another rectangle the same size as the first one. Do not draw anything in this room.

(f) Listen carefully to what your teacher tells you to do next.

G Dictation

Listen to your teacher. Write the paragraph.

It was a very strange living room. At one end there were piles of different coloured cushions thrown around the floor which was covered in a beautiful multi-coloured mat. At the other end of the room there was a huge television. Apart from that, there was nothing else! There were no chairs, sofas, tables, lamps, cupboards or anything. How did they live like that?

H Composition

1 Write a description of the Faleti family's new apartment.
- Start: The Faleti family have just moved into a new apartment. It has five rooms – two bedrooms, a bathroom, a kitchen and a living room. In the small bedroom there ...
- Explain what the furniture is, and where it is.
- Use a new paragraph for each room (but it is not necessary to describe the bathroom).

2 Draw a plan of your living room at home. Write a description of it.

Fun box

Did you know ...

... the circus in Moscow has cows that play football and dance to music?

18 Atinuke takes care

A Reading 1

Before reading: Atinuke wants to visit her friend Felicia. Look at the map and find where the two girls live.

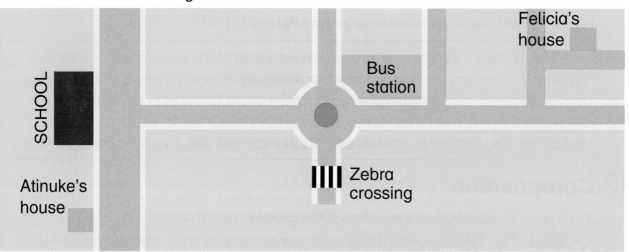

Atinuke has been invited to the house of a friend, Felicia. Atinuke has never been there before. Her mother has work to do and her father is out. Her aunt is going to walk with her.

Mother: You can go on with your aunt but you must be careful not to get lost. Aunty doesn't know where Felicia lives.

Atinuke: Don't worry, mother. Felicia's mother drew a map to show me where she lives. Look, it's very easy.

Mother: Well, let me see. Oh, yes. She's marked our house and their house. OK, you look at the map and tell me exactly where you're going to go.

Atinuke: We'll go out of our house and turn left and walk up the road to the school. We'll cross the road at the school and take the road opposite the school.

Mother: No, you won't! Haven't you learnt about road safety at school?

Atinuke: Yes, I have.

Mother: Well, then. What's the first rule for crossing the road?

Atinuke: First, find a safe place to cross. Oh, I see. If we cross in front of the school it'll be too near the corner. That's dangerous because a car could come around the corner while we're crossing. OK, we'll cross in front of our house where we can see and hear vehicles coming. Then we'll walk down the road and take the first turning on the right, opposite the school.

Mother: That's better. Go on.

B Comprehension 1

1 Why can't Atinuke's parents take her to Felicia's house?
2 What did Felicia's mother do to help Atinuke find the house?
3 What did she mark on the map?
4 Has Atinuke learnt about road safety at school?
5 What's the first road safety rule?
6 Why shouldn't Atinuke and her aunt cross the road in front of the school?
7 Where are they going to cross the road?
8 Which way will they go when they get to the school?

C Reading 2

Before reading: Give the directions from the school to Felicia's house.

Atinuke: Next we'll take the road opposite the school and then we'll go straight on and pass the roundabout.

Mother: How are you going to cross the road at the roundabout?

Atinuke: When we reach the roundabout, we'll take the road to the right and walk down there until we can cross at the zebra crossing. Then we'll walk back on the other side of the road to the roundabout.

Mother: Good.

Atinuke: We'll carry on down the road past the bus station until we find somewhere safe to cross the road.

Mother: Yes, and be very careful there because that road is very busy. You must be patient and wait until there are no vehicles coming.

Atinuke: All right. Then we'll take the second road on the left after the bus station. We'll go down there a little before we cross that road. Then we'll take the first road on the right. We'll walk down there and cross in a safe place opposite Felicia's house. There, it's not so difficult.

Mother: Remember that when you're walking in the street there'll be lots of noisy lorries and buses. They can confuse you. And you must come home before dark. It's too dangerous on the roads for children at night.

Atinuke: Of course. I'll ask aunty to collect me at five o'clock. We'll be home by half past five. Bye-bye, Mummy.

Mother: Goodbye, and please take care.

D Comprehension 2

1 Where will Atinuke and her aunt go when they reach the roundabout?
2 Where will they cross the road?
3 Why must Atinuke be very careful when she crosses the road after the bus station?
4 Which road will they take after the bus station?
5 What will they do next?
6 Where will they cross the last road?
7 Why must Atinuke go home before it is dark?
8 What time will she be home?

Word focus 🔍

Make sentences with these words:

take care   map   exactly   roundabout   zebra crossing   patient   confuse

E Grammar

1 Look. When Atinuke went to Felicia's house she got lost.

Atinuke and her aunt went **across** the road.

They went **towards** the school.

But then they went **along** the wrong road.

They went **up** a hill.

They went **down** the hill.

They went **over** a bridge.

They went **through** a market.

They went **past** the bus station.

Finally, they arrived at Felicia's house.

2 Complete the sentences with words from the box.

past	from	up	through	towards	under
over	to	down	across	along	away from

Atinuke looked carefully before she went __across__ the road.

(a) I can run much faster _____ a hill than _____ it.

(b) A river goes _____ a bridge.

(c) I wanted to catch the bus but it went straight _____ me.

(d) The dog jumped _____ the fence.

(e) I tried to catch the dog but when it saw me it ran _____ me.

(f) There is a train and a plane _____ Lagos _____ Kaduna.

(g) A tunnel can be dug _____ a mountain for a road or railway track.

(h) If you walk _____ a beach, you can find seashells.

(i) He was very thirsty so he started to run _____ the river.

3 Tell the story of Obiora's journey.

(a)

(b)

(c)

(d)

(e)

(f)

(g)

(h)

(i)

4 Write nine sentences about Obiora's journey.

F Speech

1 Ask for and give directions to each other.

ASKING FOR DIRECTIONS

> Excuse me, can you tell me the way to … , please?

GIVING DIRECTIONS

Go straight ahead.	Turn	right. left.	Then take the	first second next	turning on the	left. right.

Go past the	church. mosque. roundabout.	It's	on the right. on the left. in front of you.

2 Draw a map showing your home, your school and the streets around it. Now work in pairs. Give directions to your partner to get to your home.

G Dictation

Listen to your teacher. Write the road safety rules.

> 1 Find a safe place to cross the road.
> 2 Look left, look right, look left again.
> 3 Wait for vehicles to pass.
> 4 Walk quickly across the road.

H Composition

1 Write a letter to a friend to invite him or her to your home. Your friend knows your school but does not know where you live. Draw a simple map and give directions for your friend to get from school to your home safely.

2 Write a formal letter to the police to complain about traffic problems in your area (for example, too much traffic, vehicles travelling too fast, traffic lights not working, the difficulty of crossing the road safely).

Fun box

Can you solve this riddle?

A man rode into town on a horse. He arrived on Friday, stayed for three days and left on Friday.

How is it possible?

19 The seashell

A Reading 1

Before reading: Look at the picture. What can you see? What is happening?

Once upon a time, four sisters lived in a village near the sea. They loved the beach and the sea. They spent many days playing happily there. They collected shells, built sandcastles and ran in and out of the sea shouting with joy.

Sometimes they swam where the water was shallow. They dived to the bottom and then jumped out with a scream. However, they were careful not to go where the water was deep. Their father always said, "Don't go into the deep water because the sea is dangerous."

One day they were collecting shells. Each of the four girls made a pile of beautiful shells which they wanted to take home to give to their mother.

On the way home, Oluchi, the youngest girl, suddenly remembered that her most beautiful shell was still on a rock at the beach. She wanted to go back to fetch it. Her sisters didn't want to. It was getting dark and they were tired. They didn't want to go all the way back for one shell. However, Oluchi insisted that the shell was so beautiful that she had to go back to get it. So she went back to the beach alone.

B Comprehension 1

1 Where did the girls like to play?
2 What did they do on the beach?
3 Where did they swim?
4 Why didn't they swim where it was deep?
5 Why did the girls collect the shells?
6 Why did Oluchi want to go back to the beach?
7 Why didn't her sisters want to go back?
8 Did all the sisters go back to the beach?

C Reading 2

Before reading: Was Oluchi right to go back to the beach alone?
What do you think will happen when she gets there?

When she got back to the beach, Oluchi saw her shell lying on the rock. However, now the rock was surrounded by water. The tide had come in and all the shallow places were now deep under water. But Oluchi wanted to get her shell. She waded out into the sea to the rock. The water was almost up to her neck when she reached out and took hold of her precious shell. Just at that moment, a wave knocked her off her feet and pulled her out to sea. Within a few moments, she drowned.

When Oluchi didn't arrive home, her sisters and parents began to look for her. The whole village helped them but she could not be found. It was only three days later that the sea returned her body to the beach. Oluchi's father carried the cold body back to the village for the funeral.

The chief said that she was a beautiful girl but she died because she didn't listen to anyone and always wanted to have her own way. Everyone agreed.

D Comprehension 2

1 Could Oluchi see her shell?
2 What was different on the beach?
3 Was it easy for Oluchi to get to the rock?
4 What happened as she took hold of the shell?
5 What happened to Oluchi?
6 What happened three days later?
7 What did the chief say that Oluchi did wrong?
8 Who didn't Oluchi listen to?

Word focus 🔍

Make sentences with these words:
fetch insist surround tide wade precious funeral
have your own way

E Grammar

1 Look.

> Use an infinitive + **to** to say why we do something. This is called an **infinitive of purpose**.
>
> *Oluchi went back to the beach **to find** the seashell.*
> *We come to school **to learn**.*

2 Match each action with a purpose to make sentences.

(a) The sisters went to the beach	**(i)** to get her shell.
(b) The girls collected shells	**(ii)** to stay safe.
(c) The girls only swam in shallow water	**(iii)** to stop her returning to the beach.
(d) The older sisters argued with Oluchi	**(iv)** to give to their mother.
(e) Oluchi waded out to the rock	**(v)** to play.
(f) The villagers looked everywhere	**(vi)** to find Oluchi.

3 Write sentences with **to** + infinitive to show the purpose.

(a) Oluchi wanted to get her shell, so she went back to the beach.
    Oluchi went back to the beach to get her shell.

(b) The villagers wanted to find Oluchi, so they looked everywhere.
    The villagers looked everywhere ...

(c) Chike wanted to ask Usman a question, so he telephoned him.
    Chike telephoned Usman ...

(d) Aminat wanted to reach the top of the wardrobe, so she stood on a chair.
    Aminat stood on a chair ...

(e) Atinuke wanted a dictionary, so she went to the bookshop.
    Atinuke went to the bookshop ...

(f) Mrs Buhari needed some eggs, so she went to the supermarket.
    Mrs Buhari ...

(g) The boys were too hot in the sun, so they sat under a tree.
    The boys ...

4 Complete the sentences. Use an infinitive of purpose.

(a) Chike opened his book to do his homework.

(b) We go to school ...

(c) My father goes to work ...

(d) I go shopping ...

(e) Aminat phoned Chike ...

(f) They went to the airport ...

F Speech

1 Say the following.

When someone dies, or something bad happens to someone, we give them our sympathy. To express sympathy your voice must sound sad and serious. Use falling intonation.

I'm terribly sorry!   It's very sad!   Please accept my condolences.

2 Work in pairs. Take it in turns to be A and B.

A is Oluchi's sister or brother.

B expresses sympathy on the death of Oluchi.

3 Look at the pictures. Tell the story of 'The seashell' in your own words.

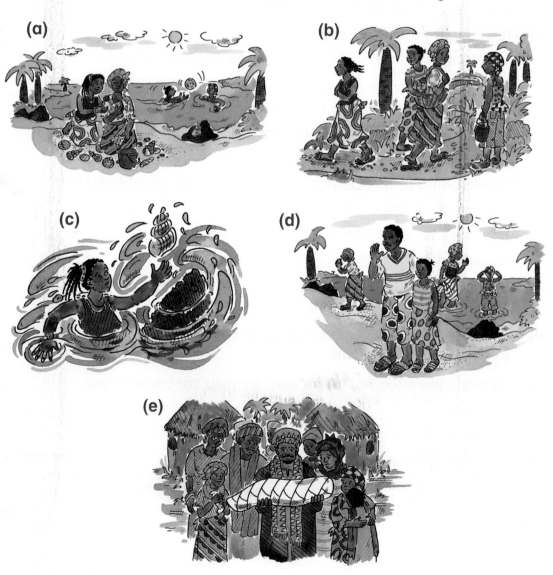

(a) (b) (c) (d) (e)

G Dictation

Listen to your teacher. Write the paragraph.

> If you can, learn to swim. Swimming is a good, healthy sport and it can save your life. The sea can be very dangerous. It is better to stay where you can keep your feet on the ground. Keep out of deep water until you can swim very well.

H Composition

1 Imagine you are one of Oluchi's sisters. Write your story. Answer the questions to help you complete the paragraphs.

Paragraph 1: We loved the sea and often played on the beach. We collected shells, ...

(a) What did you and your sisters do?

Paragraph 2: One day we were collecting shells. On the way home Oluchi remembered a beautiful shell that was on the beach. She ...

(a) What did Oluchi want to do?   (b) What did you want to do?

(c) What happened?

Paragraph 3: Oluchi did not return. We ...

(a) What did your family and the villagers do?   (b) What did you find?

(c) When did you find Oluchi's body?

Paragraph 4: We had Oluchi's funeral. ...

(a) What happened at the funeral?   (b) What did the chief say about Oluchi?

2 Write the chief's speech at the funeral.

(a) Express sympathy to the family.   (b) Explain why Oluchi died.

Fun box

Why did the chicken cross the road?	To get to the other side.
Why did the elephant cross the road?	To pick up the dead chicken.
Why did the chicken cross the playground?	To get to the other slide.
Why did the snake go to school?	To learn hiss-tory.
Why did the fool plant one naira in the garden?	To raise some money.

20 Revision B

A Reading

The Seashell
I know an old lady,
(But not very well),
And she lives in a house
That's called 'The Seashell'.
Inside there are stairs
Curling round, up so high,
You think you are on
Your way to the sky!
The house gets smaller
Nearer the top
And up in the attic
The curly stairs stop.
So it is like a shell
In a kind of way,
But you can't see the sea
Though the old lady says
When you're curled up in bed –
If you don't snore –
You can hear the sea whispering
Down on the shore.

by Daphne Lister

B Comprehension

1 Does the old lady live in a seashell?

2 Why do you think the house is called 'The seashell'?

3 Is the house near the sea?

4 Find a word in the poem which

 (a) is a name for a room at the top of a house.

 (b) describes a comfortable position to lie in bed with your legs up to your che

 (c) is to make a loud noise when you are sleeping.

 (d) describes a very quiet noise.

 (e) is another word for 'beach'.

5 Learn the poem.

C Reading quiz

1 Find the answers in the reading texts for units 11–19.

(a) What year did Gutenberg invent his printing press?

(b) Why did the boy get off the donkey in the story of 'The farmer, his son and the donkey'?

(c) What do 'congratulations' mean?

(d) When you cook pepper soup, how long should you simmer the soup for?

(e) Was Mubo's wife happy that he took a bottle of water to the chief's feast?

(f) What did Bamidele buy Fatimah?

(g) Which dowry did Fatimah accept?

(h) Where did Aminat try to hide her earrings?

(i) Where did Mrs Faleti decide to put her fridge?

(j) What is the first rule of road safety?

2 Write eight questions of your own about the reading texts for units 11–19.

3 Ask your questions.

Word focus 🔍

Make sentences with these words:

chop   disrespectful   furious   information   ingredients   insist   invent
partner   patient   squeeze   stretch   wobble

Fun box

One day a chief asked a servant to go to the market to buy him the best piece of meat. The servant brought him a tongue. The chief was very pleased.

The next day the chief sent the servant to the market again. This time he asked the servant to bring him the worst piece of meat. Again the servant brought him a tongue. The chief was not pleased this time.

"What's this?" he said. "Are you telling me that something can be both the best and the worst?"

"Well," explained the servant, "sometimes a man is very unhappy because of his tongue but sometimes his tongue makes him very happy."

"You're right," the chief said. "We must be masters of our tongue!"

D Grammar

Read. Then copy and answer.

Some of the sentences below are correct. Some are incorrect.

- For each correct one you mark with a ✓ you get 1 point. For each incorrect one you mark with a ✗ you get 1 point.
- For each incorrect sentence you can make correct, you get 2 more points. Write the corrections in your exercise book.
- Be careful! If you write a sentence which is incorrect you lose a point.

	Correct	Incorrect	Points
Chike wants a mobile phone. However, his mother thinks he is too young.	✓		1
Telegrams were used a lot and are now out of date.		✗	1
Telegrams were used a lot but are now out of date.			2

1 E-mails are used more than telegrams so they are quicker and cheaper.
2 Oluchi went back to the beach although her sisters didn't want her to.
3 Atinuke has been learning English for seven years.
4 The baby is hot because she has been cried.
5 I have finished my homework but I haven't been tidying my bedroom yet.
6 A mobile phone is used to make calls at home, at work and in the street.
7 Usman is the same old as Aminat.
8 Some gifts are as useful not as others.
9 Oluchi didn't listen to her sisters. As a result, she drowned.
10 The wave was such high that it knocked Oluchi off her feet.
11 The train went over a tunnel.
12 They went to the cinema for watch a film.
13 Atinuke bought a present to give to Hairat.

E Speech

1 Say the following sentences with the correct intonation.

(a) I was told you are getting married. Congratulations!

(b) I was told your grandmother died. Please accept my condolences.

(c) Would you like a newspaper, a magazine or a book?

2 Look at the pictures. Tell the story.

F Dictation

Look at the words in the Word focus box on page 93. Then listen to your teacher and write the dictation.

G Composition

1 Write the story of 'The three brothers' you told in Speech above.
2 Write a letter to the editor of a newspaper. Tell the editor that you think all children must be taught to swim, and why.

21 Soil

A Reading

Before reading: This is from a school textbook. How many sections are there? What are their titles?

Soil

Soil is made up of tiny pieces of rock mixed with tiny pieces of dead plants. It also contains some air and water, and minerals. Plants get their water and food from the soil.

TRY THIS ➤ **EXPERIMENT A** ▪ Take some soil and put it in a glass jar. ▪ Add water and shake it up. Then let it settle. ▪ The soil will settle in layers of different materials.	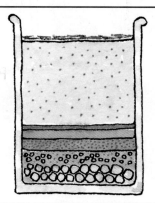

Types of soil

The tiny pieces of rock in soil hold air between them. Some types of soils have more air than others.

Clay soils have small air spaces. When it rains water can only soak into the air spaces slowly. And then the water can only drain away slowly. This makes the soil heavy and sticky.

Sandy soils are the opposite. They have larger pieces of rock and larger air spaces. Water drains through them easily; we say they have good drainage. However, this means that any minerals or goodness in the soil, which plants use as food, is washed away with the water.

Loam soils are a mixture of the other two. They have good drainage but can still hold water. They are not heavy and sticky.

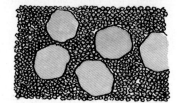

➤ **EXPERIMENT B**

- Take a handful of soil and some water.
- Add a little water and mix it in well. Make your soil moist but not wet.
- Roll the soil between your hands to make a sausage.

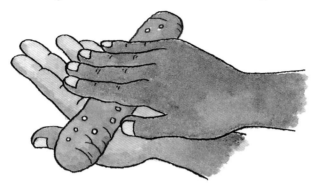

- Let it dry.
  - (a) If it stays as a sausage as it dries, it is clay.
  - (b) If it falls apart as it dries, it is loam.
  - (c) If you couldn't make a sausage because it fell apart immediately, it is sandy.

Soil and agriculture

We say a soil is *fertile* if plants grow well in it. Loam soils are the most fertile. In the rainy season clay soils are too wet and sticky because the water doesn't drain away. In the dry season they go hard and crack. Sandy soils dry out very quickly in the heat. Farmers don't usually grow crops on sandy soils; they just keep animals on them.

B Comprehension 1

Are the following statements true or false?

1 The main ingredients of soil are tiny pieces of rock and plants.
2 There are four main types of soil.
3 Water passes through clay soils quickly.
4 Clay soils are heavy and sticky.
5 Water passes through sandy soils quickly.
6 Sandy soils have lots of goodness for plants.
7 Loam soils have good drainage.
8 Loam soils are heavy and sticky.
9 Loam soils are the most fertile.
10 Farmers usually keep animals on loam soils.

C Comprehension 2

1 Why is soil important for plants?
2 What is the problem with clay soils?
3 What is the problem with sandy soils?
4 Why are loam soils the best?
5 What does fertile mean?
6 What will Experiment A show you?
7 What will Experiment B show you?
8 Do the experiments. Use soil from around your school.

Word focus

Make sentences with these words:

tiny   settle   layer   material   soak   drain   moist   roll   crack

Fun box

Match the questions and answers.

What runs but never walks?   Because they don't know how to cook.

Why do lions eat uncooked meat?   Nothing, it just waves.

What does the sea say to the beach? Water.

D Grammar

1 Look.

> Remember, we use the relative pronouns **who**, **which** and **that** to join sentences.
>
> *A farmer is someone **who** farms the land.*
> *The farm **which** we visited has very fertile soil.*
>
> **When** and **where** can also be used as relative pronouns.
>
> *I want a garden **where** there is fertile soil.*
> *I'll always remember the day **when** I first saw you.*

2 Match the two parts to make six sentences.

(a) We visited an area	**(i)** when the farmer was harvesting.
(b) We visited the farm at a time	**(ii)** where my mother was born.
(c) Did you like the restaurant	**(iii)** when Usman was outside.
(d) Chike telephoned at the moment	**(iv)** where you ate?
(e) We arrived home on the day	**(v)** where the soil was very fertile.
(f) Akure is the place	**(vi)** when I fell sick.

3 Make eight sentences from the table.

I	like	days	when	...
		times		
	dislike	places	where	
		shops		

4 Complete the sentences. Use **who**, **which**, **where** or **when**.

I like to go on holiday to a place __where__ I can swim in the sea.

(a) We usually go on holiday _____ my father is not busy at work.

(b) I have a good friend _____ wants to be a farmer.

(c) I am wearing shoes _____ are too big for me.

(d) What's the name of the boy _____ lives next door?

(e) What's the name of the river _____ flows into Kainji Lake?

(f) Farmers harvest their crops _____ the crops are ready.

(g) They always visit countries _____ the people speak English.

E Speech

1 Work in pairs. Look at the diagram. Ask and answer questions.

   What do worms do?   *They tunnel into the soil.*

2 Give a two-minute talk about '**Soil**'. Use the information in the text on pages 96 and 97, and the diagram below.

Many animals live in the soil.

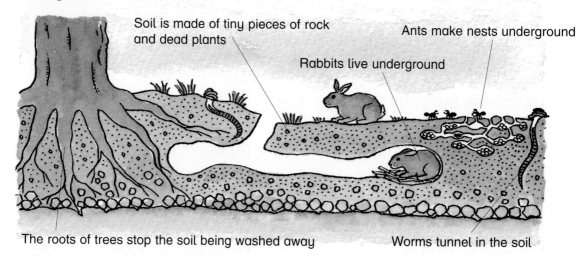

Soil is made of tiny pieces of rock and dead plants

Ants make nests underground

Rabbits live underground

The roots of trees stop the soil being washed away

Worms tunnel in the soil

F Dictation

Look at the words below. They are all in the dictation you are going to do. Then listen to your teacher and write the paragraph.

| soil   beneath   worms   beetles   insects   break down   goodness   fertile |

G Composition

Write a three-paragraph composition about soil.

Paragraph 1:

• What soil is made of

Start: Soil is made of ...

Paragraph 2:

• The three types of soil   • How they are different

• Which soil is most fertile and why

Start: There are three main types of soil. They are ...

Paragraph 3:

• What plants use the soil for   • What animals and insects use the soil for

Start: Soil is very important. Plants ...

22 The magic pot

A Reading 1

Before reading: Look at the picture. What is happening?

There was once an old woman who sold the best soup in the market. Every morning she arrived with a big black pot of hot chicken soup on her head. Then she sat down quietly under a tree and began to sell her soup. She never spoke to anyone. The village people quickly gathered around and soon the old woman's soup was finished. Immediately she picked up her pot and hurried away silently.

Kalari was a small boy who loved chicken soup. He wanted to know who the old woman was and how she made such delicious soup. One morning when the old woman put her empty pot on her head and quickly left the market place, Kalari followed her.

The old woman walked fast and they went a long, long way up a hill. Evening came and Kalari was afraid but he went on. At last the woman came to a little hut on the top of the hill and went inside.

In front of the hut stood a huge pot. Kalari carefully looked inside it. It was empty. When the woman came out of the hut, Kalari quickly hid himself. The woman went up to the huge pot and began to sing a song.

B Comprehension 1

1 What did the old woman sell?
2 Did she make the soup at the market?
3 What did the old woman do when all her soup was sold?
4 Why did Kalari follow the old woman?
5 Where did the old woman go to?
6 What did Kalari see when they arrived?
7 What was in the huge pot?
8 What did the old woman do when she came out of her hut?

C Reading 2

Before reading: What do you think will happen next? What will Kalari do?

This is the song the old woman sang:

Let's start cooking, let's start cooking
Magic pot, magic pot
Onions and tomatoes, onions and tomatoes
Chicken soup, chicken soup.

Soon Kalari could see steam coming out of the pot. When the old woman went back into her hut, he ran up to the pot. He saw that it was full of hot, thick chicken soup but when he looked under the pot he saw that there was no fire!

"I must have some of it, I'm so hungry!" Kalari said to himself. He was reaching his hand into the pot to take a piece of chicken when suddenly the old woman came out of her hut.

"Oh, you wicked boy!" she cried angrily. "Stop!"

Kalari raced down the hill. The old woman chased after him but she could not catch him. Kalari ran and ran until he reached home. Kalari lost no time in telling the villagers about his adventure.

From that day on, the old woman stopped coming to the market with her soup. Nobody went up that high hill to see her because they were afraid. But now, when people see clouds on the hill, they say, "Look! There is the steam from the magic pot."

D Comprehension 2

1 What did Kalari see when the old woman sang her song?
2 What was in the pot?
3 What did Kalari want to do?
4 What happened next?
5 Where did Kalari go?
6 What did Kalari do when he got home?
7 Why did the villagers not visit the old woman at her home?
8 Why do you think the old woman stopped coming to the village?

Word focus 🔍

Make sentences with these words:

gather around   immediately   delicious   steam   reach   chase

1 Look.

> Adjectives and adverbs make a description more interesting. They are like the colour in a picture.
>
> You can use more than one adjective
>
> a **big black** pot   a **tiny sparkling** light
>
> You can use adverbs or adverb phrases to say when, where or how something happens.
>
> *every morning*   *under a tree*   *silently*

2 Find three adjectives from the story which describe

(a) the pots   (b) the soup

3 Find five adverbs of manner (that tell how something is done) in the story.

4 Complete 'The Ant and the Grasshopper' story with adjectives and adverbs.

One **(a)**_____ day, a **(b)**_____ grasshopper was hopping about in the **(c)**_____ forest. He was singing **(d)**_____ because he liked to play. Just then, a **(e)**_____ ant walked by, carrying **(f)**_____ food he was taking home.

"Come and relax," said the grasshopper **(g)**_____ . "Don't work."

"But the **(h)**_____ winter will come soon," replied the **(i)**_____ ant. "I am storing food for then."

"There's no need to worry about winter," laughed the **(j)**_____ grasshopper. "Look around you now, it's a **(k)**_____ day. Enjoy yourself."

But the ant carried on **(l)**_____ with his work.

Then the **(m)**_____ winter came and the grasshopper was **(n)**_____ . He had nothing. He sat and watched the **(o)**_____ ants sharing out their food with each other. Then he knew that he should have worked when the days were long.

F Speech

1 Sing the magic pot song.

2 Imagine you are Kalari. Tell your family and the villagers what happened when you followed the old woman up the hill.

3 Work in pairs. Describe what is happening in the picture below.

G Dictation

Look at the words below. They are all in the dictation you are going to do. Then listen to your teacher and write the paragraph.

sigh	frightened	night	thought	sight	bright	light	staring

H Composition

Write a description of the event in the photograph above. Make your description colourful and interesting by using adjectives and adverbs. Divide it into three paragraphs.

Paragraph 1: (Start) I watched the closing ceremony of the All Africa Games in Abuja. It was …

Paragraph 2: Describe what the women were wearing.

Paragraph 3: Describe what the women were doing (the movements of the dance and why they were dancing).

23 Village and city life

A Reading 1

Before reading: Look at the picture. Where is Chike? Is he happy?

In the holidays, Chike visited his father's village for the first time.

However, Chike wasn't sure if he liked the village. There was no electricity so he couldn't watch TV. His father told him to play with his cousin, Eze.

Chike asked Eze, "What do you do here for fun?"

"We play games," said Eze.

"What sort of games do you play without electricity?" asked Chike.

Eze answered, "I play football and other sports with my friends."

Chike was in a bad mood. He said, "I don't think I could live here. I prefer city life, it's much better!"

"I disagree," said Eze. "I've been to Lagos. All you do there is watch television and play video games! What's great about that?"

"We also visit shops, parks and restaurants," replied Chike.

"Okay, I know we don't have those but we don't need them. We farm and produce our own food. I know everybody here. Everyone is my friend. Do you know everybody living on your street?" asked Eze.

"No, but I still prefer to live in a city," insisted Chike.

B Comprehension 1

1 Where did Chike go in the holidays?
2 What did Chike want to do?
3 Why couldn't he watch TV?
4 What does Eze do with his friends in the village?
5 What does Chike do with his friends in Lagos?
6 Does Chike know all his neighbours in Lagos?
7 Where does Eze prefer to live?
8 Where does Chike prefer to live?

C Reading 2

Before reading: Look at the picture. What do you think Eze and Chike will do?

The next day Chike was feeling bored.

"Come on, jump on my bike. Let's go and see one of my friends," said Eze.

"I'm not riding on that old bike! It's not safe to ride on the road on an old bike," replied Chike.

"You're frightened!" laughed Eze. "There are few cars here, no crime and the air is clean. What are you afraid of?"

"What would happen if we had an accident? If we are injured in the city, we can go to a hospital," said Chike.

"People get injured in the village and they are still alive," replied Eze.

"Yes, but what if you are seriously injured?" asked Chike.

"Well, we would have to find transport to the nearest hospital," answered Eze.

"Well, that's one point that proves city life is better than village life!" Chike said.

"Not really," replied Eze, "it's not always easy to get to a hospital in Lagos and other cities. There's often traffic jams."

"That's true! You're right about that," agreed Chike.

Eze didn't want to argue. He said, "Well, I think city and village lives are both good in their own ways. Sometimes, I love living here and at other times I want to live in a city."

"I suppose you're right, Eze. I like the quiet and clean environment here but I don't like to live without electricity," smiled Chike.

"Perhaps we could combine what we like about village and city life to make our own ideal place to live?" suggested Eze.

"I wish we could!" agreed Chike.

D Comprehension 2

1 Where did Eze want to take Chike?

2 Why didn't Chike want to go?

3 What reasons does Eze give to say life in the village is safer than in the city?

4 Why is Chike worried about having an accident in the village?

5 Why isn't it always easy to get to a hospital in a city?

6 Is Eze always happy living in a village?

7 What does Chike like about village life?

8 What do the boys agree they would like to do?

Make sentences with these words:

fun   mood   prefer   bored   crime   injure   prove   combine   ideal   suggest

E Grammar

1 Look.

Use the following expressions in a debate or argument:
- To make a point or give an opinion

I think ...	*In my opinion ...*
I believe ...	*I prefer (city life to village life).*

- To agree with a point

I agree.	*That's true!*
I think that's correct.	*You're right about that!*

- To disagree with a point

I disagree.	*Not really, because ...*
Perhaps, but ...	

2 Rewrite the sentences. Change the underlined words but keep the same meaning.

   (a) I <u>think</u> village life is boring.

      I believe village life is boring.

   (b) I <u>believe</u> life outside of the city is more healthy.

   (c) Yes, <u>I think you're right</u>.

   (d) <u>Perhaps, but</u> there are more hospitals in the towns and cities.

   (e) <u>In my opinion</u>, men are better cooks than women.

   (f) <u>I disagree with you</u>. My mother is the best cook in Nigeria!

   (g) I <u>prefer</u> food cooked by women.

3 Work in pairs. Continue the conversations. B can agree or disagree.

   (a) *A:* In my opinion, city life is better than village life.
      B: ...

   (b) *A:* I think men are better cooks than women.
      B: ...

   (c) *A:* I believe boys should wear skirts if girls wear trousers.
      B: ...

   (d) *A:* I prefer pounded yam to all other food.
      B: ...

4 Write your conversations from 3.

F Speech

Hold a class debate on the motion:

Life in urban areas is better than life in rural areas.

(a) Work in groups. Prepare all your ideas for the topic.

(b) Listen to your teacher explain how to organise the debate.

- Proposers: prepare a speech to propose the motion. Think of all the ideas you can to support it.
- Opposers: prepare a speech to oppose the motion. Think of all the ideas you can against it.
- Rest of class: think of questions to ask the speakers.

G Dictation

Look at the words below. They are all in the dictation you are going to do. Then listen to your teacher and write the paragraph.

rural	urban	preferable	unemployed	environment

H Composition

Write a composition of two paragraphs to give your opinion on life in urban and rural areas. First decide which one you prefer.

Paragraph 1: Give your opinion and your points to support your choice.

Start   In my opinion, life in _____ areas is better than life in
_____ areas. I believe ...

Paragraph 2: Give your points against the other area.

Start   I believe life in _____ areas is not so good because ...

Fun box

Did you know ...

... the first car accident was in 1896 when a car hit a bicycle?
... more people are killed every year by donkeys than die in plane accidents?

24 Aminat falls ill

A Reading 1

Before reading: Look at the picture below. What can you see?

One evening Aminat was doing her homework with Usman when she felt ill. She had to stop to rest.

"What's the matter?" asked her mother. "You don't look well."

"I'm not," she said. "I feel very weak and tired."

"Then you must go to bed immediately. You might feel better in the morning," her mother told her.

However, the next morning, Aminat wasn't feeling better. She had a bad headache and felt hot. Her mother got out the thermometer and took her temperature.

"Oh, dear," said her mother. "You've got a high temperature. I'll have to take you to see a doctor."

They took a taxi but by the time they arrived at the hospital Aminat was feeling worse. They were told to sit down and wait in the queue to see a doctor. There were lots of people waiting. One boy had crutches because he had broken his leg. A man had a bandage on his head. Some women had young babies on their laps. Some women were pregnant. Aminat liked to see the little babies but she didn't want to stay in the hospital. She wanted to go home to sleep.

B Comprehension 1

1 What happened when Aminat was doing her homework?
2 How did she feel?
3 How did she feel the next morning?
4 Why did her mother want to take Aminat to see a doctor?
5 Was the waiting area at the hospital busy?
6 Why did the boy have crutches?
7 What did Aminat enjoy while she was waiting?
8 What did Aminat want to do?

C Reading 2

Before reading: What do you think the doctor will do and say?

After some time a nurse took Aminat to see the doctor.

"Hello, Aminat. I am Doctor Okafor. What's the matter with you?" asked the doctor.

"I have a headache, my body hurts and I have a high temperature," said Aminat.

The doctor made Aminat lie down on a bed. She examined her. She listened to Aminat's heart with her stethoscope and took her blood pressure.

Then she said, "I want you to have a blood test."

Doctor Okafor sent Aminat to the laboratory. The man in the laboratory took a little blood from Aminat's finger. Then he looked at the blood with a machine called a microscope. He wrote something on a piece of paper and sent Aminat back to the doctor.

"I see," said Doctor Okafor after she read the paper. "You have malaria. You'll have to take these tablets and rest. You'll feel better in a few days."

When they got home, Aminat went to bed and took the tablets. They tasted terrible but she wanted to get better. She did get better, but she felt tired for a few days.

D Comprehension 2

1 What did Aminat tell Dr Okafor?

2 What did Dr Okafor do when she examined Aminat?

3 Where did the doctor send Aminat?

4 What did the man in the laboratory do?

5 What did the man give Aminat?

6 Who did she give it to?

7 What was wrong with Aminat?

8 What did Dr Okafor give Aminat to make her better?

Word focus

Make sentences with these words:

temperature   crutch   bandage   pregnant   heart   laboratory

E Grammar

1 Complete the sentences with words from the box.

> coughing   injection   sneezing   vomiting
> temperature   diarrhoea

(a) She's got a
_____.

(b) She's _____.

(c) She's _____.

(d) He's having an
_____.

(e) She's _____.

(f) He's got _____.

2 Complete the sentences.

> To describe a pain, only use **ache** with five parts of the body:
>
>   *headache   earache   toothache   backache   stomach-ache*
>
> With other parts of the body, use **pain**:
>
>   *I've got a pain in my leg.   The pain in my neck is worse.*

   (a) I hit my head on an open window and now I have ...

   (b) When my grandfather works in the garden he gets ...

   (c) I fell over and ...

   (d) The last time I was ill, I ...

   (e) The worst injury I had was ...

   (f) When I went to the hospital, I saw ...

F Speech

1 Work in pairs. Read the conversation. One of you is Aminat, the other is the man in the laboratory.

Man: Come in and sit down, please.

Aminat: Thank you.

Man: Hold out your hand, please. I have to take a drop of blood from your finger.

Aminat: Will it hurt?

Man: No, you won't feel much. There, it's done.

Aminat: That didn't hurt at all.

Man: I put your drop of blood on this small piece of glass which I'm now going to look at under the microscope.

Aminat: What does a microscope do?

Man: It makes things look much larger. I can see what happens in your blood. Ah! I can see the problem!

Aminat: What is it?

Man: There are some parasites in your blood. Take this piece of paper back to Dr Okafor. She will know what to do.

2 Work in pairs. Act out a conversation between a patient with a toothache and a dentist.

G Dictation

Look at the words below. They are all in the dictation you are going to do.

instruments   stethoscope   heart   thermometer   temperature   blood pressure

H Composition

1 Write your conversation between the patient and the dentist from Speech 2.

2 Read the paragraphs below. For each one, say

   (a) What is the main point?   (b) What are the supporting ideas?

> When we write a composition to explain something, we make one main point in each paragraph. This is usually the first sentence of the paragraph. Then we add a few supporting sentences to help make our point.

   Alcohol can cause many problems. People who drink a lot are not healthy. They also have no money to support their families.

3 Which of the sentences below would make a good supporting sentence for the main point?

   Main point: Smoking is dangerous to your health.
   Supporting ideas: (a) Smoking isn't good for you.
                       (b) I don't like smoking because it smells bad.
                       (c) Smoking is known to cause many illnesses.

4 Write a composition of three paragraphs on drug abuse.

   Choose two supporting sentences for each paragraph from the box below. Then write the full composition.

   Paragraph 1: Some drugs are legal and others are illegal. ...
   Paragraph 2: Illegal drugs are very dangerous for the user. ...
   Paragraph 3: Most illegal drugs are addictive. ...

   - Thousands of drug users die every year.
   - Legal drugs you can get from the pharmacy and use when you want.
   - This means that after people have used the drug once or twice, they will want more of it.
   - They will think only of drugs and will not be able to work properly or do their family duties.
   - Illegal drugs are not allowed by law so the police can arrest you if you buy, sell or use them.
   - Others go to prison.

25 The birds in the field

A Reading 1

Before reading: Look at the picture. Describe what you see. What is happening?

A mother bird had built her nest in a field of guinea corn. As the corn grew tall, she sat on her eggs. When the eggs hatched she flew around busily to find food for her chicks.

"Mother, can we always live like this?" the little birds asked her at night. "The food is good, the sun is warm, and the guinea corn smells nice when the wind blows through it."

"No, not forever," replied the mother bird. "The time will come when the farmer will harvest the field. We'll have to leave before then, or the nest will be caught by the blade of his machete."

One evening, the young birds were excited when their mother came home.

"The farmer! The farmer!" they all cried at once. "He's coming to cut down all the corn!"

The largest of the chicks explained, "The farmer and his son were in the field. The farmer said the corn was ready. He told his son to call their friends and neighbours. He said they had promised to help him with the harvest."

The chicks looked at their mother anxiously, but she only laughed.

"There's no need to worry," she said, "nothing will happen yet. If he depends on friends and neighbours, nothing will happen. Tomorrow we'll still be safe."

B Comprehension 1

1 Where was the nest?
2 What did the mother do before the eggs hatched?
3 Were the young birds happy where they lived?
4 Will the family be able to live there forever?
5 Who did the young birds hear talking in the field?
6 Who did the farmer want to call to harvest the corn?
7 Why were the chicks worried?
8 Why wasn't the mother worried?

C Reading 2

Before reading: Do you think the mother is right that the birds will be safe? What will happen?

The next evening, the mother came home and her young ones were even more upset.

"Now don't panic," said the mother bird. "What did you hear today?"

This time the middle chick spoke, "He told his son that the neighbours did not come to help. So he ordered the boy to go to the huts of all his uncles, aunts and cousins and call them to come to help harvest the guinea corn."

The little birds looked at their mother. "Do we have to go now, mother?"

"No, not yet," the wise mother replied. "If he depends on his family, nothing will happen. Tomorrow we'll still be safe."

The following evening, the babies were worried again. This time the youngest and smallest of the chicks had something to tell. "I heard the boy tell his father that the family had refused to help. They had said they were too busy. The farmer thought for a bit and then said that he and his son had to do the work themselves. He told his son to go home to collect the machetes."

"Ah, now that is different," said the mother bird. "Tomorrow morning we'll have to go. Only when a man does something himself can he be sure that it will really be done."

So the next morning they flew away before the corn began to fall.

D Comprehension 2

1 Did the friends and neighbours help to harvest the corn?
2 Were the young birds happy the next evening?
3 Who did the farmer want to help harvest the corn next?
4 Why wasn't the mother bird worried?
5 Why didn't the family help to harvest the corn?
6 Who did the farmer decide should harvest the corn?
7 What did the mother bird decide to do?
8 Why did she decide this?

Word focus 🔍

Make sentences with these words:

hatch forever blade promise anxiously depend upset panic refuse

1 Look

> Use the **past perfect** tense to talk about an earlier past. The past perfect tense is made with **had + past participle**
>
> *The mother bird sat on her eggs. Before that she **had built** her nest.*
> *I **had asked** mother for some money before I went to the shop.*
>
> With regular verbs, the past participle is made with the verb **+(e)d**
>
> *I had walked   she had climbed   they had called*
>
> However, there are many verbs which have irregular past participles
>
> *eaten   given   taken   done   made   been*

2 Make six sentences about yourself.

Before I arrived at school today I had	woken up. dressed myself. washed myself. eaten my breakfast. finished my homework. ?

3 Look at the timeline. Then match and write the sentences.

built nest	eggs hatched	corn ready	farmer asked neighbours for help	farmer asked family for help	farmer decided to harvest without help	birds left nest

EARLIER PAST ←——————— ——————→ PAST   NOW

(a) Before the birds left the nest,

(b) Before the farmer decided to harvest without help,

(c) Before the farmer asked his family for help,

(d) Before the farmer asked his neighbours for help,

(e) Before the corn was ready to harvest,

(f) Before the eggs hatched,

(i)   the eggs had hatched.

(ii) he had asked his family for help.

(iii) the mother bird had built her nest.

(iv) he had asked his neighbours for help.

(v) the farmer had decided to harvest without help.

(vi) the corn was ready to harvest.

F Speech

1 What is the moral of 'The birds in the field'?

(a) A bird in the hand is worth two in the bush.

(b) The early bird catches the worm.

(c) If you want something important done, do it yourself.

2 Work in pairs. Think of a story teaching one of the morals above.
It can be a story you already know or you can make one up.
Make notes on your story to help you remember it.

3 Tell your story to another pair.

4 Hold a class debate on the motion:

A farmer does the most important job in the country.

(a) Work in groups. Prepare all your ideas for the topic.

(b) Listen to your teacher explain how to organise the debate.

- *Proposers:* prepare a speech to propose the motion. Think of all the ideas you can to support it.
- *Opposers:* prepare a speech to oppose the motion. Think of all the ideas you can against it.
- *Rest of class:* think of questions to ask the speakers.

G Dictation

Look at the words below. They are all in the dictation you are going to do.
Then listen to your teacher and write the paragraph.

trust	however	rely	expected	assist	unless	depend

H Composition

1 Write the story you told in Speech above.

2 Write a short composition of two paragraphs to give your opinion on the importance of farming. Give your opinion and some points to support this.

Fun box

Did you know ...

... a bird of prey is a bird that kills and eats other birds and animals?

... the largest bird of prey is the condor of South America which has a wingspan of 3 metres?

26 Family

A Reading 1

Before reading: Look at the picture. What is happening?

Mrs Okocha is the sports teacher in Atinuke and Aminat's school. She blew her whistle and the game started. The ball flew down the right-hand side of the netball pitch.

"Aminat!" Atinuke called out to her friend. Aminat looked over. Atinuke pointed to the sideline.

"Watch the ball! Keep your eyes on it!" Mrs Okocha yelled at them.

Aminat looked to where Atinuke pointed. There was a crowd of people standing on the side of the pitch. Aminat could see her parents, her brother Usman and their friend Chike. Atinuke's aunts, an uncle and her parents were also there. Some of their friends had also stayed after school to cheer on their team. They were all shouting and screaming for the girls to encourage them.

After the match, the girls were very happy. They had won the match but, most of all, they were delighted that their friends and families had been there to support them.

"I love my family, they always come to support me," said Atinuke.

"Mine too," replied Aminat.

"We're lucky, aren't we?" said Atinuke.

"Yes, we are!"

"Why do you girls think you are lucky?" interrupted Mrs Okocha.

"We're lucky because our parents support us and they provide for us."

B Comprehension 1

1 What game were Aminat and Atinuke playing?
2 What were Usman and Chike doing?
3 Why did Mrs Okocha shout "Watch the ball!" at the girls?
4 Who were the girls looking at?
5 Why were the girls' families watching the game?
6 When was the game played?
7 Did Aminat and Atinuke's team win the game?
8 Why do the girls think they are lucky?

C Reading 2

Before reading: List ways in which parents support and provide for children.

"What do your parents provide for you?" Mrs Okocha asked.

"Clothes, shoes and pocket money, for example," said Atinuke.

"That's good. Remember that they also provide you with good food such as fish, vegetables, fruit, meat and cereals to give you a healthy diet and make you grow," said their games teacher.

"Yes, they also take care of us when we are sick. When I had malaria, my mother took me to the hospital and my father bought me medicines. They nursed me until I was well again," said Aminat.

"That's good. In addition, they provide you with a safe place to grow up. They work really hard so that you can both live in lovely homes," said Mrs Okocha.

"We know," said the girls.

"They also make sure that you attend school so that you know how to read and write," said Mrs Okocha.

"I had a big birthday party and my parents bought me a new dress," said Aminat.

"A family whose members support, help and encourage each other is a strong family. You two have good families so you must both respect them and be good girls," said Mrs Okocha.

D Comprehension 2

1 Make a list of all the things the girls and Mrs Okocha say parents provide and do for children.
2 What does Mrs Okocha say makes a strong family?
3 What does she say Aminat and Atinuke have to do?

E Grammar

1 Look.

> The past perfect tense is made with **had + past participle**.
> With regular verbs, the past participle is made with the verb **+(e)d**
>   *Their friends **had stayed** after school to watch the game.*
> However, there are many verbs which have irregular past participles
>   *drunk   got   won   drove   seen   built*

2 Listen to your teacher explain how to play past participle bingo.

3 When Chike went to school yesterday he left his bedroom like this:

When he arrived home yesterday afternoon his mother had tidied up.
What had she done?

4 Write eight sentences about what Chike's mother had done.

She had turned off the light.

120

F Speech

1 Play the game *Just a minute* in groups of five.

> my family members   my mother   my father   my brother   my sister
> my uncle   my aunt   my cousins   my grandparents   my home

- You each have to speak for one minute about one of the topics in the box.
- Look at the full rules of the game on page 54.

2 Recite this poem.

When I went out one day,
My head fell off and rolled away.
When I saw my head had gone,
I picked it up and put it on.

When I got into the street
Someone cried, "Look at your feet!"
I looked at them and sadly said
I'd left them both asleep in bed!

G Dictation

Look at the words below. They are all in the dictation you are going to do.

> education   attend   fees   equipment   encourage   support   activities

H Composition

1 Write a composition on the needs of the family.

Include some of these things in your composition:

- housing
- food and clean water
- clothing
- health care
- education

> Remember that each paragraph should have a main point and one or two supporting ideas.

Start: All families need proper housing. We need a roof over our heads to protect us from the weather and keep us warm. Without proper housing, babies and children will get sick.

2 Write a letter to your parents to thank them for what they provide for you.

27 Water

Reading 1

Before reading: Look at the diagram. What does it show?

Water is everywhere. The sea covers 71 per cent of the world. There are also lakes and rivers and there is water in the air and in the clouds above.

Have you noticed that water is usually moving (and when it stops moving it soon become dirty and full of insects)? There is a huge movement of water called the water cycle – see the diagram below.

The water cycle

The water runs along streams and rivers into the sea. The sun warms the water. Some of the water changes into gas (or vapour) and rises to make clouds. We say the water *evaporates*. When the clouds become full and the temperature changes over the land, the vapour turns back into water. Rain falls. We say the vapour *condenses*. The rain runs into small streams and then bigger rivers. It flows into lakes or the sea. The water cycle continues.

B Comprehension 1

1 How much of the world is covered by water?
2 What happens when water stops moving?
3 Where do rivers flow to?
4 What happens when the sun warms the sea?
5 What happens when the clouds are full and the temperature changes?

C Reading 2

Before reading: Name five things you use water for.

We need water to live. We use it for so many things, for example drinking, washing and watering crops.

We have to make sure there is enough water for people, crops and farm animals. So we build dams on rivers to make a large lake, or reservoir. We can then take water from the reservoir to use for ourselves and to irrigate the land.

Water is also a source of power. Have you ever put your finger over the end of a tap or a pipe when water is running? Try it – you will feel the force of the water pushing your finger. This force is used to make hydro-electric power. When a lot of water goes through a dam it can be used to make electricity.

Over a third of the electricity in Nigeria comes from hydro-electric power. Our biggest hydro-electric power station is at the Kainji dam across the River Niger in Niger State. Lake Kainji is a huge lake created by the dam.

1 What happens when we build a dam on a river?

2 What do we use water from a reservoir for?

3 What do you feel if you put your finger over the end of a tap?

4 What can be produced when water goes through a dam?

5 How much of Nigerian power comes from water?

Word focus

1 Match the words and their meanings

(a) stream	(i) a wall built across a river to hold back the water
(b) reservoir	(ii) a lake used as a store of water
(c) evaporate	(iii) to put water onto fields to make things grow
(d) condense	(iv) another word for a gas
(e) vapour	(v) a small river
(f) dam	(vi) to change from liquid to vapour (water to vapour)
(g) irrigate	(vii) to change from vapour to liquid (vapour to water)

2 Make sentences with these words:

cycle   source   force   power

E Grammar

1 Look.

Questions in the past perfect tense

Had	I you he/she/it we they	+ past participle ...?		Yes,	I you he/she/it	had.
				No,	we they	hadn't.

Had the water filled the reservoir?   Yes, it had.

2 Usman won a school prize for English at the end of Primary 3.

He won it because	he had studied hard.
	he had learned a lot of new words.
	he had done all his homework.
	he hadn't played around in class.

Work in pairs. Ask and answer about Usman.

A: Had he studied hard?   B: Yes, he had.

3 Write questions and answers.

(a) Aminat had played well. Had Aminat played well?
                                          Yes, she had.

(b) Chike had stayed behind to watch the game.

(c) The parents had come to support the girls.

(d) The girls had won the game.

(e) Mother hadn't prepared supper.

(f) The children had lost their way.

4 Complete the sentences. Put the verbs in the past simple or past perfect tenses.

> Remember, when we describe two events in the past we use the past perfect tense for the earlier one.

(a) By the time I (arrive) at school, the lesson (start).

   By the time I arrived at school, the lesson had started.

(b) My mother (be) late so the game (start).

(c) By the time I (wake up), my mother (go out).

(d) Before the police (arrive), the thief (run away).

(e) Yesterday I (meet) a man who (be) at school with your father.

(f) When my mother (arrive) home, we (be) ill because we (finish) all the ice cream.

5 Write five sentences about what you had done by the time you were eight years old.

   By the time I was eight, I had read many books.

Fun box

Did you know ...

- ... you can boil water? It changes to steam.
- ... you can freeze water? It changes to ice.
- ... one litre of water weighs exactly one kilogram?
- ... there is no water on the moon?
- ... ships travel faster in cold water than in warm water?

F Speech

1 Work in pairs. Take it in turns to describe the water cycle. Use the diagram on page 122.

2 Work in a group of four. Share all the information you can on water.
- List all the things you used water for yesterday.
- List any other use of water you can think of.
- Where does the water you use come from? How does it get to your home?
- List the main rivers and lakes of Nigeria.
- Note down anything you know about the Kainji dam and Lake Kainji. (Where they are, when the dam was built, their size, etc.)

G Dictation

Look at the words below. They are all in the dictation you are going to do. Then listen to your teacher and write the paragraph.

| salt | oceans | fresh | streams | frozen | ice | Arctic | Antarctica |

H Composition

1 Write three paragraphs about water. Use the information you talked about in Speech above.

2 Imagine there is a problem with the water in your area, for example
- there's not enough for people to drink and wash with
- there's no water for irrigation
- there's too much water and it's flooding homes
- it's dirty

Write a formal letter to the Manager of the State Water Corporation to complain.

28 Favourite foods

A Reading 1

Before reading: What is your favourite food? Why is it so good?

It is Sunday tomorrow. Atinuke is getting very excited. She loves to shop with her mother on Saturdays. She also loves Sundays because of the special lunch that they usually have at home.

"Shall we do our shopping now?" she asked her mother.

"I haven't got enough money at home. Let's wait for your daddy to come home. He's gone to the bank," said Mother. "What do you children want to eat tomorrow?"

"Rice and chicken," shouted Atinuke.

"Why rice? I prefer pounded yam," said Tunji, Atinuke's younger brother.

"Rice is better," said Atinuke firmly.

"I disagree," replied her brother.

"What do you know? I'm older than you!" Atinuke said angrily.

"What has our age got to do with pounded yam and rice?" asked Tunji.

Atinuke thought for a second before replying, "Nothing, but I know that all my friends prefer rice to pounded yam."

"Then they don't know what they're missing. Pounded yam is simply the best in my opinion, especially when eaten with egusi soup," said Tunji.

"I don't agree," argued Atinuke. "You can make rice in different ways. There is jollof rice, fried rice, coconut rice and rice pudding but you can only make pounded yam as pounded yam."

"Pounded yam is stiff and very filling. You can have it with any soup of your choice like ewedu, egusi, spinach and ogbono," said Tunji.

"Children," laughed Mother, "Stop this argument now."

B Comprehension 1

1 What day did this conversation take place?
2 Why couldn't Atinuke and her mother go shopping?
3 Why do you think Atinuke's father went to the bank?
4 Is Tunji older or younger than Atinuke?
5 What did Atinuke and Tunji argue about?
6 What does Tunji prefer to eat with pounded yam?
7 Which different ways of cooking rice does Atinuke talk about?
8 Was mother angry with the children for arguing?

C Reading 2

Before reading: Which is easier to prepare and cook – rice or pounded yam?

Tunji and Atinuke were too excited now to stop their argument.

"I prefer rice because it is light and can be eaten with a spoon or fork," said Atinuke.

"Yes, just like you can eat pounded yam with a spoon or with a fork and knife," replied Tunji.

"Oh no, I'm sure you'll agree that pounded yam tastes better when eaten with your fingers."

"True, but you can't eat rice with okro or ogbono soup you know," laughed Tunji.

"I'm sure some people do," said Atinuke.

Tunji squeezed his face in disgust and said, "Yuck! Both soups are too slimy for rice! They are perfect for pounded yam."

Atinuke hadn't finished her argument yet, "It's much easier to cook rice than pounded yam. You only need a pot to cook rice for fifteen minutes. For pounded yam you need to peel and cook the yam, pound it with a mortar and pestle to become smooth and stiff before you eat it. If you don't pound it well, it will be lumpy."

"You know what?" interrupted their mother.

"What?" they both asked.

"We're going to make some rice and some pounded yam," she said. "Grandma is visiting tomorrow and she loves pounded yam."

"Grandma, daddy and I are going to eat pounded yam," said Tunji happily.

"Mum and I prefer rice, and that's what we're going to eat," smiled Atinuke.

D Comprehension 2

1 Why didn't the children stop arguing?
2 Why can rice be eaten with a spoon or fork?
3 Does Tunji agree that pounded yam is better when eaten with your fingers?
4 Why does Tunji think you can't eat rice with ogbono soup?
5 What do you need to cook rice?
6 What do you need to pound yam?
7 What happens if you don't pound yam well?
8 How does mother stop the argument?

Word focus 🔍

Make sentences with these words:
special   firmly   stiff   filling   disgust   slimy   lumpy   mortar and pestle

E Grammar

1 Look.

Phrasal verbs are made up of a main verb and another word:
   look after   look up   go up   carry on   give up
It is not always possible to understand the meaning of these by looking at the meaning of each word.
   *I have to **look after** my little sister.*
You know the meaning of **look** and **after** but this does not tell you that **look after** means **take care of**.

2 Match the two halves of these sentences.

(a) Obi got up   (i)   with your work.

(b) You can look up   (ii) sugar.

(c) I want you to carry on   (iii) from Nguru last night.

(d) They got back   (iv) at six o'clock this morning.

(e) You have to fill in   (v)   the word in the dictionary.

(f) Oh no! We've run out of   (vi) your name and address on the form.

3 Replace the underlined phrasal verbs with a verb from the box.

enter   return   discover   collect   continue   wait

(a) Turn left here and then <u>go on</u> until the end of the road. The church is just there.   continue

(b) Can you <u>give back</u> my dictionary, please?

(c) We must all <u>pick up</u> some rubbish after school.

(d) We will have to <u>hold on</u> a minute, he's not ready.

(e) I will <u>find out</u> the truth when I collect in your books.

(f) You can <u>go in</u> when you're ready.

4 Complete these sentences.

The price of yams will _____go_____ up again soon.

(a) Your bedroom is very untidy! Please go and _____ up now.

(b) I'm sorry I'm late. The bus _____ down on the way to school.

(c) You look tired. What time did you _____ up this morning?

(d) I want to listen to the news. _____ on the radio, please.

(e) When are you going to _____ back the money I lent you?

5 Make sentences using the phrasal verbs.

(a) carry on   Let's carry on with our work while the teacher is outside.

(b) get up

(c) give up

(d) take off

(e) turn off

(f) tell off

F Speech

List the favourite foods to eat with stew or chicken in your area. Then choose two to hold a class debate on. For example

Pounded yam is better than rice.

Work in groups. Prepare all your ideas for the topic.

- *Proposers:* prepare a speech to propose the motion. Think of all the ideas you can to support it.
- *Opposers:* prepare a speech to oppose the motion. Think of all the ideas you can against it.
- *Rest of class:* think of questions to ask the speakers.

G Dictation

Look at the words below. They are all in the dictation you are going to do.

| healthy | balanced | diet | protein | fat | carbohydrate | vitamin |

H Composition

Write a composition giving your opinions on which basic food (e.g. rice or pounded yam) is better. Give your opinions on

- the taste
- how many ways it can be cooked
- what it can be eaten with
- how long it takes to prepare and cook
- how it is eaten

You can use some of the expressions in the box.

I believe ...   I think ...   In my opinion ...   I prefer ...

On one hand, rice can be cooked in many different ways.
On the other hand, pounded yam can be eaten with many different soups.

It is clear/true that rice is easier to prepare than pounded yam.
I am sure everyone will agree that rice is quicker to cook than pounded yam.

However, pounded yam can be eaten with many different soups.
Although rice can be cooked in many ways, pounded yam can be eaten with many different soups.

29 Practice makes perfect

A Reading 1

Before reading: What do your parents say if you do well in exams? What do they say if you do badly?

Emeka is Chike's older brother. He sat the Common Entrance exam in May. His father promised to buy him a present if his exam result was good.

"If you get a good result, I'll buy you a new bike," his father told him.

On the day the exam report arrived, Emeka was not in. His father looked angry as he flung the result on the table.

"Look! Emeka did badly in his exams," he said loudly to Chike's mother.

Chike stopped playing his video game. He listened to his parents as they discussed Emeka's result. His mother left what she was doing and picked up the results. "I'm disappointed," she said. "He should have done better. If he had studied harder, he would have passed the exam."

"He watches too much TV," said his father. "If he had done well, I would have bought the bike for him as I promised."

"I'm going to have a word with him when he arrives," said his mother.

Immediately Emeka came in, Chike wasted no time in telling him. "Dad got your result," he whispered.

"Great!" said Emeka. "If I have a good result, I'll get a new bike."

B Comprehension 1

1 What present did Emeka's father promise him?
2 What must Emeka do to get the present?
3 What was Chike doing when the results arrived?
4 Did Emeka do well in his exams?
5 What should Emeka have done to pass the exam?
6 What does Emeka's father think Emeka does instead of studying?
7 Is Emeka going to get the new bike?
8 Did Emeka know he had a bad result?

C Reading 2

Before reading: What do you think Emeka's mother will say to him?

"You can forget about the new bike," said Chike.

"Are the results bad?" asked Emeka.

"Well, he's angry that you didn't do better," answered Chike.

Emeka was sad. He looked down and started to cry.

"I'm sorry," said Chike. "I wish I hadn't told you."

Their mother walked in and saw Emeka.

"Why are you crying?" she asked.

"He's sad because of his poor result," answered Chike.

"Emeka, there is no point in crying," said their mother. "If you had worked harder, you would have passed your exams. It's obvious that you didn't study well. You told me last week that your team lost the football match at school because they didn't practise enough. If they had practised, they would have played better than the other team and they would have won. That's the way it is with anything you do. Practice makes perfect."

"Mum, I'm sorry," said Emeka quietly. "I promise to do better next year."

D Comprehension 2

1 Why was Emeka's father angry with him?

2 What did Emeka do when he learned the news?

3 Why did Chike say, "I wish I hadn't told you"?

4 Why was it obvious that Emeka didn't study well?

5 Why didn't Emeka's football team win the match?

6 If the team had practised more, what would have happened?

7 What is the lesson that Emeka's mother is teaching?

8 What is Emeka going to do in the future?

Word focus 🔍

Make sentences with these words:

exam   result   fling   discuss   disappointed   obvious   practise   perfect

E Grammar

1 Look.

> To talk about something which is possible, or likely to happen, use
>
> **If** + present simple tense, **will** + infinitive
> **If** *you get a good result, I* **will** *buy you a new bike.*
>
> To talk about something which is unlikely to happen, use
>
> **If** + past simple tense, **would** + infinitive
> **If** *I found some money, I* **would** *buy a new bike.*

2 Complete the sentences.

(a) If it rains tomorrow, I will ...

(b) If it snowed tomorrow, I would ...

(c) I will be happy if ...

(d) I would be happy if ...

(e) You'll ... if ...

(f) You'd ... if ...

3 Look.

> To talk about something which is impossible, which cannot happen, use
>
> **If** + past perfect tense, **would have** + past participle
> **If** *I had worked harder last year, I* **would have** *passed my exam.*

4 Match the two parts to make sentences.

If + past perfect tense	*would have* + past participle
(a) If Emeka had worked harder,	(i) I would have scored in the basketball game.
(b) If I had been taller,	(ii) I would have taken my Common Entrance exam this year.
(c) If Chike had known Emeka would be sad,	(iii) he wouldn't have told him about the bad results.
(d) If I had been older,	(iv) he would have passed his exam.

5 Complete the sentences.

(a) If I had worked harder, I would have ...

(b) If I had been older, ...

(c) If I had been taller, ...

F Speech

Imagine you are visiting a secondary school for the first time. A teacher is going to ask you some questions. The questions will be about

- you (your name, age, etc.)
- your education (your primary school, your best school subjects, etc.)
- your interests (your hobbies, sports, etc.)

Work in pairs.

(a) Write ten questions the teacher can ask.

(b) Take it in turns to ask and answer the questions.

G Dictation

Look at the words below. They are all in the dictation you are going to do. Then listen to your teacher and write the paragraph.

| worked | passed | be pleased | bought |

H Composition

1 Complete the form below about yourself.

Family name		Other names	
Postal address			
Age	Height		Weight
School name			
School address			
Favourite school subjects			
Favourite sports			
Hobbies			

2 Write a formal letter to the head teacher of a secondary school. Give the information about yourself that you talked about in Speech above.

A Reading

What is under?

What is under the grass, Mummy,
what is under the grass?
Roots and stones and rich soil
where the loamy worms pass.

What is over the sky, Mummy,
what is over the sky?
Stars and planets and boundless space,
but never a reason why.

What is under the sea, Mummy,
what is under the sea?
Weird and wet and wondrous things,
too deep for you and me.

What is under my skin, Mummy,
what is under my skin?
Flesh and blood and a frame of bones
and your own dear self within.

by Tony Mitton

B Comprehension

1 Each verse of the poem has a question and answer. What are the four questions?

2 The ends of the 2nd and 4th lines of each verse rhyme. What are the four pairs of rhyming words?

3 Read the poem in pairs. One of you read the questions, the other the answers.

> **Word focus** 🔍
>
> **Make sentences with these words:**
> boundless   weird   wondrous   skin   flesh   frame

C Reading quiz

1 Find the answers in the reading texts in units 21 to 29.

(a) The three main types of soil are clay, loam and _____ .

(b) How do we describe soil in which plants grow well?

(c) What was the name of the boy in *The magic pot*?

(d) Where did Eze want to take Chike on his bike?

(e) Where in the hospital did the man who took blood from Aminat work?

(f) What was the moral of the story *The birds in the field*?

(g) How much of the world is covered by water?

(h) What verb means to put water onto fields to make things grow?

(i) What does Mrs Okocha teach?

(j) Who told Emeka that he had received bad exam results?

2 Write eight questions of your own about the reading texts in units 21 to 29.

3 Ask your questions.

Word focus 🔍

Make sentences with these words:

moist   combine   urban   sore   blade   promise   depend
refuse   expect   cheer   encourage   interrupt

Fun box

Find the answer to this riddle.

My first letter is in house, but not in mouse.
My second letter is in hot, but not in hat.
My third letter is in like, but not in bike.
My fourth letter is in win, but not in won.
My fifth letter is in day, but not in say.
My sixth letter is in ago, but not in go.
My seventh letter is in may, but not in mad.
My whole means no school. What am I?

D Grammar

Read. Then copy and answer.

> Some of the sentences below are correct. Some are incorrect.
> - For each correct one you mark with a ✓ you get 1 point. For each incorrect one you mark with a ✗ you get 1 point.
> - For each incorrect sentence you can make correct, you get 2 more points. Write the corrections in your exercise book.
> - Be careful! If you write a sentence which is incorrect you lose a point.

	Correct	Incorrect	Points
I have to look after my little sister.	✓		1
The old woman made soup in a black huge cooking pot.		✗	1
The old woman made soup in a huge black cooking pot.			2

1 I hate places when it is very noisy.

2 What's the name of the boy who hit you?

3 She made hot delicious chicken soup.

4 A grasshopper was playing happily in the dark forest.

5 In my opinion, women are better cooks than men.

6 I prefer urban life is best.

7 I've got an armache.

8 She has a sore throat.

9 Before the eggs hatched, the mother bird sat on the eggs for two weeks.

10 The birds only left the nest when they had heard the farmer decide to cut the corn himself.

11 By the end of the hot season, the river was evaporated.

12 When I got home, my mother had tidyed up my toys.

13 Had they stayed after school to watch the netball game?

14 By the time I had arrived at school, the lesson started.

15 If it snows tomorrow, I would be very surprised.

16 If I had run a little faster, I would have won the race.

E Speech

1 Work in pairs. Talk about what you are going to do in the holidays.

2 Look at the pictures. Tell the story.

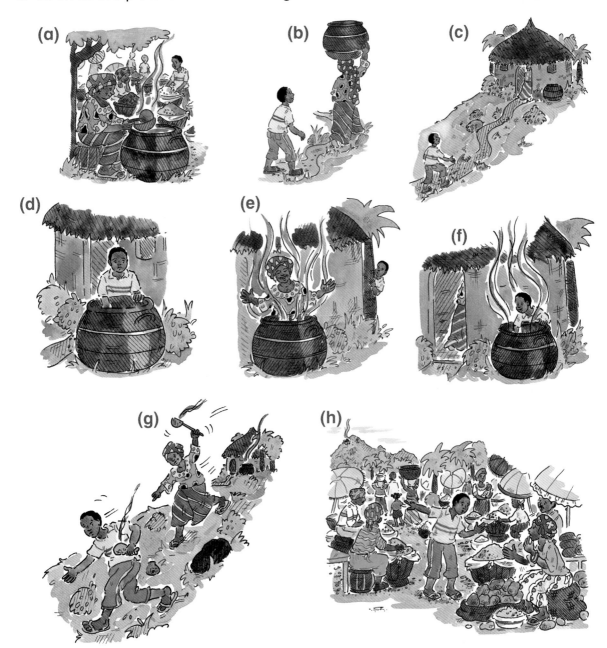

(a) (b) (c) (d) (e) (f) (g) (h)

F Dictation

Look at the words in the Word focus box on page 137. Then listen to your teacher and write the dictation.

G Composition

1 Write the story of 'The magic pot' you told in Speech above.

2 Write a letter to a friend about what you are going to do in the holidays.

Irregular verbs

Base form	Simple past	Past participle	Base form	Simple past	Past participle
become	became	become	hold	held	held
begin	began	begun	hurt	hurt	hurt
bend	bent	bent	keep	kept	kept
bite	bit	bitten	kneel	knelt	knelt
bleed	bled	bled	know	knew	known
blow	blew	blown	lay	laid	laid
break	broke	broken	leave	left	left
bring	brought	brought	let	let	let
build	built	built	lie	lay	lain
burst	burst	burst	lose	lost	lost
buy	bought	bought	make	made	made
catch	caught	caught	mean	meant	meant
choose	chose	chosen	pay	paid	paid
come	came	come	put	put	put
cost	cost	cost	read	read	read
cut	cut	cut	ride	rode	ridden
dig	dug	dug	ring	rang	rung
do	did	done	rise	rose	risen
draw	drew	drawn	run	ran	run
drink	drank	drunk	say	said	said
drive	drove	driven	see	saw	seen
eat	ate	eaten	sell	sold	sold
fall	fell	fallen	set	set	set
feed	fed	fed	shake	shook	shaken
feel	felt	felt	shoot	shot	shot
fight	fought	fought	shut	shut	shut
find	found	found	sing	sang	sung
fly	flew	flown	sink	sank	sunk
forget	forgot	forgotten	sit	sat	sat
freeze	froze	frozen	speak	spoke	spoken
get	got	got	spend	spent	spent
give	gave	given	spread	spread	spread
go	went	gone	stand	stood	stood
grow	grew	grown	steal	stole	stolen
hang	hung	hung	stick	stuck	stuck
have	had	had	sting	stung	stung
hear	heard	heard	swim	swam	swum
hide	hid	hidden	take	took	taken
hit	hit	hit	teach	taught	taught

Base form	Simple past	Past participle	Base form	Simple past	Past participle
tear	tore	torn	wake	woke	woken
tell	told	told	wear	wore	worn
think	thought	thought	win	won	won
throw	threw	thrown	write	wrote	written
upset	upset	upset			

The verbs **be** and **have** are very irregular. Here are their full forms:

be

Simple present: I am
You are
He is
She is
It is
We are
You are
They are

Simple past: I was
You were
He was
She was
It was
We were
You were
They were

Present participle: being

Past participle: been

have

Simple present: I have
You have
He has
She has
It has
We have
You have
They have

Simple past: I had
You had
He had
She had
It had
We had
You had
They had

Present participle: having

Past participle: had

Word list

A
accept
achieve
action
activity
admire
adventure
agriculture
ankle
Antarctica
anxiously
apartment
appreciate
arable
Arctic
argue
arrange
assist
at the end of
at the far/other end
attend
attic

B
balanced
bandage
beef
beetle
bend down
beneath
bicycle pump
billion
blade
blame
bookcase
boundless
boxing
braid
brake
branch
breath
bright
bubble

C
carbohydrate
celebrate
chalk
challenger
character

chase
cheat
cheer
chick
chief
chop
circle (v)
clay
cocoa
collect
combine
comfortably
communication
computer operator
condense
condolences
confuse
contents
copy
corner
cough
couple
crack
create
crime
crowd
crutch
curled up
cushions
cutlass
cycle

D
dam
definition
delight
department
depend
design
detergent
deviation
dial
diarrhoea
diet
disappointed
discuss
disgust
disrespectful
diver
double

dowry
drain
drama
dried
dye
dying

E
each side of
earrings
education
electricity
e-mail
encourage
engineer
enthusiastic
equipment
evaporate
exactly
examination
expect

F
fair
fault
feast
fee
fertile
fetch
filling
firmly
flesh
fling
fold
force
forever
formality
frame
freeze
fresh
fun
funeral
furious
further

G
gather around
gears
gift
giggle
gloves
goat

graduation
grin
guess
guest

H
handlebars
handsome
hatch
have one's own way
heart
hesitation
hobby
hole
housewarming
hurry
hydro-electric

I
ideal
immediately
in addition
incident
independent
infectious
inform
information
ingredients
injection
injure
inner tube
insist
instrument
intend
intention
Internet
interrupt
invent
invitation
irrigate

J
jewellery
joke
judge
juice

K
kind

L
laboratory
lake

layer
lemon
loam
loss
lumpy

M
machete
manage
map
mark
material
measles
medium-sized
member
message
method
microscope
mirror
mixed
mobile
moist
mood
mortar
multi-coloured

N
notice (v)

O
obvious
occasionally
opposite
optional
organise
out of date

P
pain
palm wine
panic
park (n)
pass by
pastoral
patient (adj)
pattern
pedal
perfect
pestle
pile
pitch
plan (n)
plan (v)
plough
pour
power
practice (n)
practise (v)

precious
pregnant
prevent
print
promise
protein
proverb
provide
pump (v)
puncture
purpose
put someone through

Q
queue

R
radio signal
rash
ray
rear (v)
recover
reed
refuse
relax
remove
repeat
repetition
replace
reply
result
rinse
roll
roundabout
RSVP
rubber patch
rudely
runny
rural

S
saddle
sandcastle
sausage
scene
scientist
secret
settle
shore
sideline
sigh
sight
silver
simmer
skin
slimy
smart

sneeze
snore
soak
soil
sore
source
spare
special
squeeze
stare
steam
stethoscope
stiff
stir
store
stranger
strap
stretch
string
stripe
suffer
sufficient
suggest
suit
support
surround
sympathy

T
take care
tear to pieces
telegram
telegraph
temperature
tender
text
thermometer
thorn
tide
tightly
tiny
tiptoes
tractor
traditional
treat
trust
tunnel (v)
twisted
tyre
tyre lever

U
unable
unemployed
unscrew
unsightly

unskilled
unwilling
unwind
unwrap
upheaval
uphill
upset
urban
useful

V
vapour
vet
video game
vitamin
vomit

W
wade
wardrobe
watch (n)
weird
wicked
wire
wobble
wondrous
workspace
worm

Y
yell

Z
zebra crossing

143

Macmillan Education
Between Towns Road, Oxford, OX4 3PP
A division of Macmillan Publishers Limited
Companies and representatives throughout the world

www.macmillan-africa.com

ISBN: 978-9780-18337-0

Designed by Kamae Design
Illustrated by Martha Hardy, Beehive Illustration and Margaret Welbank and Jenny Williams, Linda
Rogers Associates
Cover design by Macmillan Publishers Limited
Cover illustration by Jenny Williams, Linda Rogers Associates

The publishers would like to thank the following schools for their participation
in the development of this course:
Eduland Children's School, Lagos
High Tree International School, Lagos
Oluyole Private School, Ibadan
Richmab International School, Ibadan
First Choice Children School, Owerri
Premier International School, Kano

We would like to acknowledge Catherine Adenle for her
contribution to the development of the reading passages
in the following Units: 1, 3, 8, 9, 13, 16, 23, 26, 28, 29.

The authors and publishers would like to thank the following for
permission to reproduce their material:
David Higham for the poem "What is under" from *Plum* by
Tony Mitton; Macmillan Boleswa for the extracts from
Chamber-Macmillan SA Dictionary for Senior Primary

If any copyright holders have been omitted, please contact
the publishers who will make the necessary arrangements
at the first opportunity.

The authors and publishers would like to thank the following for
permission to reproduce their photographs:
Adire African Textiles: Duncan Clarke p4. Alamy: Douglas Peebles p42(br), Sarkis Images p42(crb).
Corbis: Wolfgang Kaehler pp27, 42(bl), Annebicque Bernard p42(cl), Charles E. Rotkin p50(b),
John Madere p64, Jim Craigmyle p97(bl), Carl and Anne Purcell p97(bc), Corbis RF pp42(blt), 97(br),
Wendy Stone p112, Ed Kashi p126. Getty Images: Stone pp42 (crt), 43(tr,tl), 51(bl), AFP p104,
Taxi pp 50(tr), 51(tr). www.tropix.co.uk: Richard Ashford p123

Printed and bound in Malaysia

2009   2008   2007
10 9   8   7   6   5